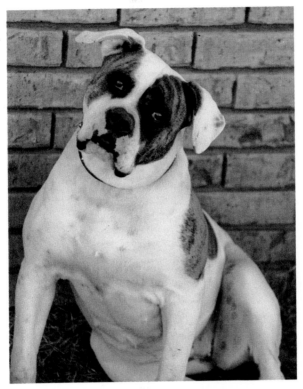

Blackwell's Black-Eyed Susan, owned by the author John Blackwell.

American Bulldogs
KW-221

Photography: Bob Barber, John Blackwell and Isabelle Français.

Drawings: Scott Boldt, Richard Crammer, Richard Davis, AnnMarie Freda, Scott Holwick, E. Michael Horn, Andrew Prendimano, John Quinn, and Alexandra Suchenka.

Title page: The new kid on the block—the American Bulldog is a sound and biddable guard dog. Owner, Louis Maldarelli of Palisades, NY.

The text of this book is the result of the joint efforts of the author and the editorial staff of T.F.H. Publications, Inc., which is the originator of all sections of the book except the chapters dealing with the introduction to the breed, the breed standard, and grooming. Additionally, the portrayal of canine pet products in this book is for general instructive value only; the appearance of such products does not necessarily constitute an endorsement by the author, the publisher, or the owners of the dogs portrayed in this book.

© **Copyright 1994 by T.F.H. Publications, Inc.**

Distributed in the UNITED STATES to the Pet Trade by T.F.H. Publications, Inc., One T.F.H. Plaza, Neptune City, NJ 07753; distributed in the UNITED STATES to the Bookstore and Library Trade by National Book Network, Inc. 4720 Boston Way, Lanham MD 20706; in CANADA to the Pet Trade by H & L Pet Supplies Inc., 27 Kingston Crescent, Kitchener, Ontario N2B 2T6; Rolf C. Hagen Ltd., 3225 Sartelon Street, Montreal 382 Quebec; in CANADA to the Book Trade by Macmillan of Canada (A Division of Canada Publishing Corporation), 164 Commander Boulevard, Agincourt, Ontario M1S 3C7; in the United Kingdom by T.F.H. Publications, PO Box 15, Waterlooville PO7 6BQ; in AUSTRALIA AND THE SOUTH PACIFIC by T.F.H. (Australia), Pty. Ltd., Box 149, Brookvale 2100 N.S.W., Australia; in NEW ZEALAND by Brooklands Aquarium Ltd. 5 McGiven Drive, New Plymouth, RD1 New Zealand; in Japan by T.F.H. Publications, Japan—Jiro Tsuda, 10-12-3 Ohjidai, Sakura, Chiba 285, Japan; in SOUTH AFRICA by Multipet Pty. Ltd., P.O. Box 35347, Northway, 4065, South Africa. Published by T.F.H. Publications, Inc.

Manufactured in the United States of America by T.F.H. Publications, Inc.

AMERICAN BULLDOGS

John Blackwell

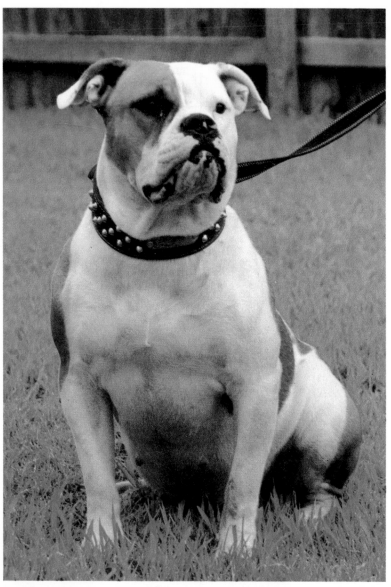

This worthy bitch is Blackwell's Ida Red owned by the author.

Contents

WHAT IS THE
AMERICAN BULLDOG? 6

THE BLUEPRINT OF THE
AMERICAN BULLDOG 16

THE STANDARD FOR THE
AMERICAN BULLDOG 29
Standard of Perfection for the American Bulldog

SELECTING YOUR DOG 33
Where to Buy; Pet or Show Dog; Male or Female; Adult or Pup; What to Look for in a Puppy; Pedigree and Registration

THE NEW FAMILY MEMBER 49
Advance Preparation; Finding a Veterinarian; Children and Puppies; Be a Good Neighbor; Getting Acquainted

FEEDING REQUIREMENTS 59
The Puppy's Meals; Comparison Shopping; Developing Good Eating Habits; Feeding Guidelines

ACCOMMODATIONS 69
The Dog Bed; The Crate; The Dog House; Cleanliness; Exercise; Exercising for You and Your Dog; Nylon Discs; Polyurethane Flexible Floppy Flying Discs; Tug Toys; Balls

HOUSEBREAKING AND TRAINING ... 87
Housebreaking; Patience, Persistence, and Praise; Training; When and How to Train; The Collar and Leash; Giving Commands; Some Specific Commands

BEHAVIOR MODIFICATION 101
Problems with the Barking Dog; Aggressive Behavior and Dominance; Destructive Tendencies

HEALTH CARE 112
Swallowing Foreign Objects; What Toys Are Safe for Dogs?; If Your Pet Swallows Poison; Danger in the Home; Vehicle Travel Safety; Protect Yourself First; Administering Medicine; In Case of an Accident; Protecting Your Pet; Inoculations; Distemper; Canine Hepatitis; Leptospirosis; Rabies; Parvovirus; Lyme Disease; Parainfluenza; External Parasites; Internal Parasites; Canine Senior Citizens

PREVENTIVE DENTAL CARE 138
All Dogs Need to Chew; Natural Chew Bones; Rawhide Chews; Nylon Chew Devices; Floss or Loss; The Importance of Prevention; Canine Dental Breakthrough

BREEDING 153
The Female "In Season"; When to Breed; Choosing the Stud; Preparation for Breeding; The Female in Whelp; Preparing for the Puppies; Whelping; Raising the Puppies; Weaning the Puppies; The Decision to Spay or Neuter

DOGS AND THE LAW 172
Buying and Selling; Dogs as Property; General Guidelines for Dog Owners; Travel; Cruelty; Landlords and Dogs

INDEX 190

What is the American Bulldog?

The American Bulldog holds a place unique in the annals of purebred dogs. It is just now being discovered and introduced to the public. Most people are still unaware of its existence, and it is being treated like a "new" breed. In fact, the American Bulldog is an ancient breed once thought to have become extinct. It is the *original* breed called "Bulldog" and is the ancestor of many of today's popular breeds.

When a dog lover looks at old paintings and lithographs of Bulldogs, from about 1850 on back, he is looking at pictures of the American Bulldog. When histories of other breeds mention the "Bulldog" as one of its ancestors, they are generally talking about the American Bulldog.

One of the first questions that comes to mind when considering the American Bulldog is its name. If this breed is really so old, how did it come to be named "the American Bulldog" instead of simply "Bulldog"? Simple! The name was already taken. Well, if that's so, why was it taken and how did that happen?

In order to understand fully how this dog got his present name, we need to think, for a moment, of just how the breed came to be in the first place.

England during the Middle Ages was a tough place to live, as

Johnson's King Kong photographed in 1950—over 125 pounds of pure power. John D. Johnson says he was "the best dog I ever owned."

was most of the world. There was little time for the working class to develop hobbies or pursue leisure activities. The upper classes might have been able to amuse themselves with breeding dogs for their pleasure, but the rest of the world kept dogs only if they proved useful in their daily work. The cattle drovers and butchers kept dogs that could help them control and catch their cattle. Every place that developed a cattle industry developed, over the years, a dog that could do just that—catch cattle. In England that dog came to be known as the Bulldog. One thing that these butchers' dogs had in common was that, regardless of the country in which they developed, they all seem to have sprung from mastiff stock and they all seemed to weigh well over a hundred pounds.

The organization of the "sport" of bull-baiting in the year 1204 probably instituted the conscious breeding of Bulldogs with the goal of developing a dog better suited to this pursuit than other dogs randomly bred. Prior to this time, the dogs were kept solely for their actual assistance of the butcher in his daily work, but once bull-baiting began to take on the importance of a spectator sport, the dogs had some "extra" value. Human nature being what it is, it is only reasonable to assume that since there was now a contest

Ida Red as a toddler . . . and a cute one at that.

between the dogs and the bulls, and between the dogs themselves, wagering would ensue. The Bulldog now had a value to "outsiders," and the pups from better performing dogs would certainly fetch a better price. Actually, any price would be an improvement since there wasn't much commerce in dogs at the time.

Well, the Bulldogs were being bred with some thought given to the probable outcome of possible matings. Breeding theories weren't very scientific but at least there was some thought and effort

What is the American Bulldog?

to breed dogs better than their parents, and more attention was given to breeding dogs to others of the same type.

While we consider this, let's not get too carried away and think for a moment that his lot in life was one whit improved. The Bulldog's value was directly linked to his ability to fight bulls, and by now other large animals like bears and

Ignorance was the rule of the day, medical care was unknown even for people, and all animal life was regarded far less than even the lowly consideration people gave to each other. A dog that was injured or fell ill either recovered on its own or it died. The Bulldogs that survived were a pretty hardy lot. Over the centuries, they produced a dog

Johnson's Rose II and Johnson's Tosh both weigh in at 85 pounds and are supreme protectors.

lions, and his ability and willingness to endure pain. To this end, he was often brutalized to demonstrate his ability to suffer willingly. These demonstrations often resulted in a dog's death, but they certainly enhanced the price of his puppies.

It should also be remembered that compassion for one's fellow man was not at an all-time high.

whose iron constitution became almost legendary.

The breed continued along its "merry" way until the early part of the 1800s. The world was becoming a little more civilized, a little more genteel in its pleasures, and a little more compassionate in its treatment of animals. Bull-baiting, along with dog fighting, was outlawed.

An important early bitch, Sandman's Golden Lady—75 pounds worth of action and power from years past.

The law against dog fighting had little effect on the Bulldog, the "sport" having been taken over by a dog more suited to its demands: the cross between the Bulldog and several aggressive terriers, the bull-and-terrier. The outlawing of bull-baiting was another matter altogether. With no legitimate outlet for his talents, the Bulldog fell into the limbo of the forgotten and was soon found no more in his native land.

The move against blood sports was accompanied by a period of general increase in the average person's living standard and time available to devote to interests other than mere survival. Exhibitions of dogs in shows became popular, and dogs began to be bred with their primary purpose in life being able to win at these dog shows.

The Bulldog, as he was in those days, was not particularly impressive in appearance and was not held in high regard by the general populace. Some breeds, such as the Irish Wolfhound and Scottish Deerhound, had been favorites of the noblemen and had long and romantic histories behind them. Other breeds, like the Irish and English Setters, had long been favored sporting dogs for

What is the American Bulldog?

wealthy landowners to amuse themselves with in their pursuit of game birds. The Bulldog had no such influential body of backers. He was the dog of the lower working class—a brute suited only for the sweaty and bloody task of aiding in the slaughter of animals destined for the tables of the masses. He was, in fact, somewhat of a quarrelsome fellow; and parading a number of these dogs around in the same ring might have provided more excitement than the show promoters had in mind.

Johnson's Rose I—by any other name, she is still one dynamic bitch.

The dog shows were provided with a "show" Bulldog for exhibition by crossing the Bulldog of that day with the Pug. This little alteration was performed widely from about 1835 until about 1865. The resultant dog made an excellent Bulldog for the shows. He was not only a handier size than the original but he looked much more impressive with his exaggerated width and breadth combined with a lower profile and a broader, more imposing-looking head. He also displayed a much milder temperament.

With the advent of the dog shows came the necessity of categorizing the dogs into distinct breeds. Clubs rapidly formed to promote individual breeds and pedigrees, and registration of dogs soon followed. It only stands to reason that one of the primary requirements in showing, promoting, and registering a breed is a breed name. Since the show-type Bulldog was a product of the actual working Bulldog, which breed was not going to be promoted by any group, the name "Bulldog" was ideal. Thus the name "Bulldog" was awarded to a cross-breed dog created specifically for showing at the dog shows, and the dog we commonly call the "English Bulldog" continues to be known by this name today.

The show-type Bulldog attracted an army of enthusiastic

followers and eventually even became the National Dog of England. Although he was never used in any capacity in any blood sport, he came to be a symbol of British tenacity worldwide. The original Bulldog quietly slipped into oblivion in his native land. Had it not been for the immigrants to the colonies, who brought some of their dogs with them, the story of the Bulldog would have ended.

England, during the early 1700s, was suffering through some pretty grim economic times. The prisons were filled with people unable to pay their debts. A plan was put forth whereby certain debtors would be allowed their release from prison if they would immigrate to the new colony of Georgia. This land had been obtained by Oglethorpe from the Creek Indians.

The settlement idea would serve England in two ways. First, it would provide a buffer between England's holdings in Virginia and the Carolinas and the French in New Orleans and the Spanish in Florida. It would also relieve the Crown of the responsibility of feeding the debtors in the prisons.

Although no debtors were ever released to go to Georgia, the new colony was settled by many eager members of the working classes who were barely able to survive in England and leaped at the chance for a new life in America. Many of these settlers

Suzie takes the first ever Best in Show for an American Bulldog! Owner, John Blackwell.

brought all their possessions with them, including their dogs. A fair number of these dogs were the working Bulldogs of the day, a time before the rise of dog shows and the demise of bull-baiting. The Bulldogs they brought were the original, common Bulldogs.

These early settlers were frontiersmen in every sense of the word. The land had to be cleared and the settlements protected from unfriendly Indians, the French, and the Spanish. Life was full and busy; survival a full-time occupation. Once again the big plantation owner might indulge

What is the American Bulldog?

himself with a small kennel of bird dogs or a pack of foxhounds. The class of people who kept Bulldogs kept them for their usefulness and nothing more.

By the time dog shows came to America and the American Kennel Club (AKC) was formed, America had suffered through the Civil War. New York, Boston, and Philadelphia were the centers of commerce and culture, with Chicago a sort of muscular cousin on the edge of the frontier. The South was looked upon as poor, uneducated, and backward. Southerners were thought of as a bunch of "hillbillies."

There was no effort to include any of the various breeds of dogs indigenous to the South into the fold of the AKC. Foreign dogs from foreign lands were considered chic; dogs in the South were just considered common. Since the AKC already had a dog called "Bulldog," another name would have to be found to avoid confusing the general public if the "Bulldogs" of the South were to be recognized outside their native areas, but there was little interest in promoting the dogs anyway. Actually, they were often called various

names to differentiate them from the show-type Bulldog; old-time Bulldog, working Bulldog, pit-Bulldog, and fighting Bulldog were all used at one time or another, as were Southern White, Old-Fashioned White, and Georgia Giants, to describe what we now call the American Bulldog.

If you think I have exaggerated the situation with dogs indigenous to the South, then why aren't you, and the rest of the world, familiar with the Mountain Cur or the related Black Mouth Cur? How about the Lacy Cowdog or the

Bulldog Drummond, owned by Kyle Symmes of Temecula, CA, is a Schutzhund dog, boar hunter and family guard.

A foundation dog of John D. Johnson, this is Sandman the Great.

What is the American Bulldog?

The infamous Dick the Bruiser, Johnson's 95-pound hero, a foundation sire and an all-time favorite Bulldog.

July Hound? The Plott Hound and the Catahoula Leopard Dog are finally getting some recognition, but they have all been a part of the South for many years.

The Bulldog was also known throughout the South, but he had never been considered a fashionable breed and there had never been any effort to organize the breeders into a club or register the individual dogs themselves. There were actually very few people who could claim to be breeders anyway.

American Bulldogs are not nearly as aggressive towards other dogs as American Pit Bull Terriers, but they are by nature assertive, dominant animals, and they will not stand for another dog to challenge their dominance. American Bulldogs are often kept along with other dogs, but not with dogs that are likely to "get in their face," so to speak. Most of the rural people who kept a Bulldog did just that, they kept "a" Bulldog. Some would keep a pair, dog and bitch, and some might save a young bitch from the litter of an old one, but few indeed were the people who tried keeping two males for any length of time, or more than two bitches for that matter.

The fast and agile Rose II, owned by the author.

No, the Bulldog was preserved through the years by individuals who needed their services and liked their character. A neighbor down the road might see what a good Bulldog can do and decide to get a pup and eventually breed a litter and pass them along to his neighbors and kinfolk, but there were no kennels, as we think of them, raising Bulldogs.

I think at this point thanks are in order to John D. Johnson, who is primarily responsible for preserving the remnants of this fine breed from being lost forever.

The Blueprint of the American Bulldog

When discussing AKC-recognized breeds of dogs, it is a fairly simple matter to describe the dog under discussion. All breeds recognized by the AKC are described in detail by a written "Standard of Perfection." The mainstay of the AKC is their sponsoring of dog shows and awarding titles of excellence, called championships, to those dogs that win a prescribed number of awards against a prescribed number of competitors at a prescribed number of shows. The dogs are judged by comparing each competitor against the "ideal specimen" of that breed as described by the "Standard." The dog that comes closest in appearance to the dog detailed by the standard will be the winner.

This system was originally designed to ensure that those dogs which were the closest representatives of the breed, and the physically soundest, would be used for breeding, and the breed would therefore continue to look like it was supposed to look. As good as this idea sounds, it does not always work to the betterment of the breeds involved.

When dog shows first began, almost all breeds displayed a wide variety of types within each breed. These variances were due to regional differences, sloppy breeding practices, and individual preferences. The problem with dog shows was that instead of saying that this group of dogs, within a breed, fell within the acceptable range according to the standard, they said that one

Multi-Best in Show winner Suzie (or Blackwell's Black-Eyed Susan) is a fine example of desirable type.

particular dog was a better specimen than another. Even in those cases where the standard was written with a broad enough range of acceptable features, the final judging was done by a person, and people have individual preferences. Human beings are very competitive by nature, and if a certain dog, or type, began to win more than an average share of the shows, the majority of the breeders would breed to him or his type. In short order, all the winning dogs of a breed began to resemble each other very closely. This naturally led to consistency of type that renders all variations as inferior.

Breeding dogs with the primary goal of winning at dog shows not only excludes variety within a breed but it also leads to exaggeration of the breed's features. If a 27-inch Doberman looks more impressive than his 26-inch competitors, and wins a lot, it is only reasonable that a 28-inch dog is going to look even more impressive. You shouldn't be surprised when I tell you that I have seen several Dobermans over 30 inches. This trend towards exaggeration has led to unmanageable coats on Cocker Spaniels, tall gawky Irish and English Setters that can't hunt and have no endurance, Great Danes so tall and skinny that they rank as the clumsiest dogs on earth. The real problem with dog shows

An American Bulldog living in Australia.

is that they reward physical appearance over mental soundness or "livability."

Since the American Bulldog has been fortunate enough to avoid this lessening of his true nature and ability, he is a far better family dog than most of us are used to, but his physical description can vary widely.

American Bulldogs can be as short as 21 or 22 inches at the shoulder, or as tall as 26 or 27 inches. I've seen them weigh as little as 80 pounds and as heavy

The Blueprint of the American Bulldog

as 140. These sizes are for mature males; the bitches will be considerably smaller. I've seen females as small as 60 pounds and I have one that weighs just over 100, and I've seen pictures of some bitches that look even larger.

While there can be quite a variance between individual dogs, the average American Bulldog can be described as follows: a muscular dog of medium height. The head is roughly box-shaped, fairly large for the size of the dog, but not excessively so. The muzzle is also box-shaped; fairly broad, deep, and relatively short. An undershot bite with the teeth

Blackwell's Rock N' Roll, Roxie, is owned by Jay and Linda Jerchau of Tulsa, OK, and weighs 80 pounds.

not visible is preferred, but an even or scissors bite is allowed. The even bite is more powerful, but many stockmen prefer a dog with an undershot bite.

The body is deep and broad, but not to the point of exaggeration. The back is short, giving the American Bulldog the look of a fairly stocky, powerful dog; quick on his feet and in his movements. He is very quick in a short distance and able to turn and spin with remarkable quickness and agility. Although giving the impression of a powerful dog (which he certainly is), he does not do it by exaggeration of any part of his physical makeup. His hindquarters are moderately angulated, broad, and muscular. His front legs are equally muscular, with well-defined muscles in his forearms, but there is no hint of bowed legs or crookedness in his front end. He is a sound, powerful, balanced heavyweight in the range of medium-sized dogs.

Color has never determined a dog's working ability. Consequently, no color is preferred over another. It is a matter of personal choice. The colors available are solid white, solid brindle (in any shade), brown, tan, and pied. The most common color, and my preference, is a predominately white dog with patches of color (usually a shade of brindle). I have never seen a solid-colored dog, that is, one without at least a little white on the muzzle or chest. Two coat colors you will not find on an American Bulldog are black-and-tan, and fawn (or brown) with a black mask.

A final feature of the American Bulldog is his tail. It is moderately long, is often carried above the back, and often ends in a complete curl. A short tail that ends at or before the hock joint, the so-called "pump-handle" tail is often found in dogs with a high percentage of Pit Bull Terrier blood. It is *not* desirable in the breed.

Some American Bulldogs are quite stocky while others are lighter and more athletic in appearance. Some heads are quite broad, with massive skulls and short, broad muzzles. Others will display heads of moderate size with longer, less heavy muzzles. This variety within the breed is one of the reasons that some people have questioned its purity of breeding.

It is my belief that the American Bulldog is a pure breed. It is my belief, too, that it is the same breed used in England for almost a thousand years as a butcher's helper, combatant in the bull ring, and described by dog writers for centuries. I do not believe that the breed has been "created" by blending various other breeds in fairly recent times as some

Terminator in lean condition at 18 months of age.

knowledgeable dog writers have suggested. Now that I have stated my position so no one can misunderstand me, let me say that I am sure that there are some American Bulldogs that have been crossed with other breeds fairly recently.

Most of the general public, and almost all newcomers to the dog fancy, believe that a registration certificate from a kennel club means that the dog in question is a purebred. They also think that the names appearing on a dog's pedigree are actually his ancestors. Ninety-nine-and-nine-tenths percent of the time they are correct in their assumptions, but the old-timers in the dog game know that there has always been, and will always continue to be, some fudging going on.

There was a Boxer kennel in the Chicago area during this breed's heyday that produced great numbers of puppies sired by a top-winning champion dog. This dog was also used by breeders from around the country who shipped their bitches to be bred to this great dog. An interesting thing

A pair of eight-month-old American Bulldogs from Australia. World-wide interest grows steadily in the breed.

was eventually noted. This dog seemed to be siring four or five litters each week (for quite a long period of time), and although the kennel also kept three other adult males on the premises, none of them ever appeared on a pedigree. Draw your own conclusions.

People are given to experimentation, and dog breeders are always trying to find some way to improve their own stock and better the other guy. Sometimes the introduction of an outside dog is well documented, sometimes not. It is common knowledge among Mastiff breeders that the breed was, for all practical purposes, extinct in

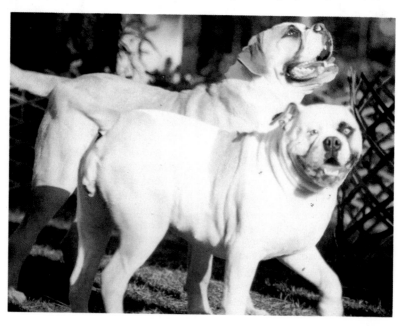

England at the end of World War II and that the dogs that were produced in the years following that war quite often resembled Great Danes, Bloodhounds, and St. Bernards. An occasional pup still turns up with a rather long coat. In fact, the Kennel Club of Great Britain allowed that a dog could be bred to an unregistered dog, even one of another breed; and the pups bred back to the

breed can quickly be eradicated to a great extent with intelligent breeding.

If responsible dedicated dog breeders will bring in another breed to help them achieve their desired goals, then are we to be so naive as to assert that no farmer ever bred this dog to one of another breed and passed the pups off as the real thing? Well, I've lived in the rural South and I

Inquisitive and intelligent, Bulldog pups cannot be ignored.

parent breed; and these pups bred back to the parent breed; and after three such breedings, the resultant pups could be registered as purebred dogs of that parent breed. This practice was allowed not too long ago and may still be allowed for all I know. Actually, it is a good way to introduce desired traits into a breed; the influence of the other

know how people actually act.

I can see the owner of a good male Bulldog letting him run loose and breeding whatever female he also happened to have around. These pups would likely be given to friends and neighbors and

The Blueprint of the American Bulldog

Johnson's Bruiser Bo, weighing in at over 135 pounds, was a famous early Bulldog.

probably be called Bulldogs. The males would grow into adulthood and breed whatever they happened to come across, and the pups wouldn't look much like Bulldogs anymore. It is possible that the bitch pups might be taken to be bred by a Bulldog when they matured, and those pups would certainly be pretty Bulldoggy.

It is easy to see that with the bitch pups from a Bulldog crossbreed there was a possibility of breeding back into the breed. The male pups would just tend to dissipate their bloodlines into the pool of mongrels in the area. The pure Bulldog bitches were another matter. It would be very unlikely for the owner of a Bulldog bitch to allow her to breed with any dog

other than another good Bulldog. This is how the breed would maintain its purity through the years—through the bitches.

Once a few people began to maintain Bulldog kennels, the purity of breeding was assured. Assured, that is, if all the breeders kept accurate records and didn't try any experiments of their own.

In discussing American Bulldogs with others, I have heard three different breeds mentioned as possible building blocks from which the American Bulldog could have been formed. There were the English Bulldog, the Bullmastiff, and the Pit Bull Terrier.

One noted dog scholar, whose opinion I respect very much, has offered his opinion that the American Bulldog is a newly created breed comprised from the blending of the three breeds mentioned. On paper this looks plausible, but it fails to take into account the evidence that there were certainly Bulldogs identical with today's American Bulldog in the early years of this century.

John D. Johnson said that his father acquired his first in 1903. My father has often told me stories about his Bulldog, Queenie, that was identical to my own dogs today. Dad got Queenie in 1915 or thereabouts. I encountered the huge Bulldogs myself in the 1940s and again in 1955, although I didn't know at the time what they were. Since there are written descriptions and painted representations of Bulldogs identical to today's American Bulldogs from the 1800s, 1700s, and earlier, it seems very unlikely that he is a blend of breeds that his own history antecedes.

Well, if the American Bulldog isn't newly created, perhaps it has been newly "enhanced." The most common speculation is that the very large size of some American Bulldogs is the result of Bullmastiff crosses into their bloodlines. Once again, it seems logical but it's highly unlikely.

Anyone who has actually been involved in any breeding program knows how very difficult it is to introduce new characteristics into a line and have them reproduce consistently. They also know that along with the desired characteristics, they are going to get a number of unwanted ones. Breeding these out while retaining the desired features can be almost, if not actually, impossible.

A study of the standards of perfection for any number of breeds can verify what I have just said for those of you who have not tried to breed dogs for a number of generations and create a "line."

Any breed that has been developed from a mixture of other breeds will have a list of physical traits which should be considered disqualifying in the show ring, and dogs with these faults should

never be used for breeding. Different breeds will have different taboos, but the common thing about most of them is that the disqualifying feature is something that will show the dog's link to one of his parent breeds.

American Staffordshire Terriers cannot be all white or more than 80 percent white. The reason is that one of its ancestors (the original Bulldog) was often primarily white. The founding breeders wanted to establish the Staff as a breed in its own right and disassociate it from the Bulldog. They also ban black-and-

Johnson's Tosh, at 85 pounds, is a swift, solid mover.

tan because the terrier side of that equation was often black-and-tan. There are plenty of other examples, but my purpose is to show that only a total, concentrated effort by all parties involved can hope to eliminate the evidence, and even then it's not wholly effective. Any Am Staff breeder knows that an occasional mis-colored dog will still be born in even the most tightly controlled breeding program.

With this information, and considering the fact that most Bullmastiffs are fawn with a black mask, we can look at the question of Bullmastiff blood in the American Bulldog with a new perspective. Where are the fawn-with-black-mask American Bulldogs?

The fawn-with-black-mask coloring is one of the most common in the dog kingdom. We've all seen hundreds of such dogs. Many mongrels are this color. Even brindle Bullmastiffs produce them. I am sure that if Bullmastiffs had been used, even slightly, in a breeding program to increase the size of American Bulldogs, there would be some fawn-with-black-mask pups born every now and then. I've never seen nor heard of one, but we banned that color in the standard just in case one ever shows up. There are some other differences in the two breeds that also don't show up in the American Bulldog,

but I think that the color question should satisfy.

Some people wonder why, if there is no Bullmastiff in the American Bulldog, are some of them as large as a Bullmastiff? The fact is that Bulldogs of well over a hundred pounds are a historical fact, and with today's better knowledge of nutrition, we are all getting larger. Making size the primary goal of a planned breeding will also have the effect of producing more large dogs.

The show-type, or English, Bulldog has been mentioned as a possible contributor to the American Bulldog, but there is no evidence to support the idea. Most supporters of the American Bulldog look upon the other dog as a mere toy. Many consider it a joke. There would be no advantage to breeding to the "English" except to reduce the size of the American and produce a lower, blockier dog. Some American Bulldogs are fairly low and blocky, but not as blocky as the show dog.

I have never seen an American Bulldog undershot to the extent you would expect from a cross with old sour-mug, and American Bulldogs have a nice long, distinctive tail. A cross with the bow-legged dog would certainly produce at least a small percentage of corkscrew tails. So much for the English Bulldog theory.

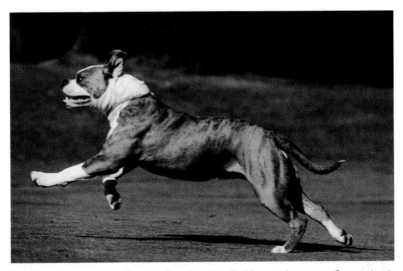

Reach and drive . . . and power describes this Bulldog on the move. Owner, Louis Maldarelli.

The third breed often mentioned as a possible cross into the American Bulldog bloodlines is the American Pit Bull Terrier. I'm afraid that this has been a fact in some cases.

Some of these crosses have been inadvertent and unknowing; others are deliberate attempts to modify the American Bulldog into a similar but different dog.

Because of the variety of names by which the American Bulldog has been known, some confusion has been inevitable. The American Bulldog has been known as the Pit Bulldog in some areas and was registered under that name until recently. The American Pit Bull Terrier also has

been called a Pit Bulldog, or simply Pit Bull, and quite a few people don't know the difference.

The American Bulldog was not registered by any kennel club until fairly recently. One of the assurances that your dog is purebred is the fact that most kennel clubs won't register a dog unless both his parents have been registered. This is a pretty logical requirement but not at all workable when you are just beginning to register a breed. Since, at one time, there were no American Bulldogs registered at all, it follows that none would have registered parents and none would be eligible for registration. Some leeway is obviously called for.

The Blueprint of the American Bulldog

The procedure for the two registering bodies has been to require a written pedigree, if one was known, and a statement from the dog's owner that the dog was purebred, to his best knowledge. Often, pictures of the dog in question were required. This seems about the only way you are going to get any dogs registered at all for some time. Once the registration process has been in effect for 20 or 30 years, there should be enough registered dogs whose parents have been registered for five or six generations and the books can then be closed to any unregistered dogs. In the meantime, a lot can happen. It is a very simple matter to breed your bitch to any dog of your choosing and put any dog you want on the registration application as the sire of the litter if neither parent is registered in the first place.

I bought some puppies from an established breeder some years back. This person is a professional man and raises a few litters as a hobby. One of his gripes about the public's lack of knowledge about American Bulldogs is that many people often think his dogs are just big Pit Bull Terriers. This man gets very upset that someone might think that he is raising dogs that have had so much bad publicity. Well, I amused myself by getting six-generation pedigrees made up for my pups and guess what? I recognized some of the names in the fifth and sixth generation as American Pit Bull Terriers. I raised the breed for over ten years and knew the names I was seeing on my American Bulldog pedigree.

Here is a case of a man unwittingly breeding from a line of dogs with mixed blood. I'm absolutely sure that he was unaware that there was any Pit Bull Terrier in his dogs' background, but there it was. It appears that someone bred his Pit Bulldog with a "Pit Bull" and thought that they were the same breed. When

Johnson's Incredible Mean Machine proved an important producer for the breed.

asked to fill out a pedigree form, they listed the correct dogs, so I don't see any attempt to deceive anyone, just an honest mistake. This man's line has been used by quite a number of people breeding American Bulldogs.

I doubt that mistakes like the one above were very common. But I'm sure that, considering the

Bulldog from a line of dogs I had seen and liked. I wouldn't just rely on the enthusiasm of the breeder.

There is another factor that could possibly encourage some introduction of Pit Bull Terrier into the American Bulldog. There is a segment of American Bulldog breeders that is promoting a "performance"-oriented Bulldog.

Johnson's "boss dog", this is Aristocrat on the trail.

average uneducated dog owner, they did occur. Considering the fact that the Pit Bull Terrier is half-Bulldog to start with, and the position of the Kennel Club of Great Britain towards cross-breeding, I doubt that this type of mistake has affected the American Bulldog to any appreciable degree, but I would be careful to get my American

These breeders promote their dogs as being "stronger, faster, more agile, and able to whip any other breed of dog"; they are especially adamant that "their" dogs are superior to the "other" American Bulldogs. The "other"

Terminator participates in a Schutzhund protection demonstration . . . muscles at work.

does not necessarily mean that these dogs are smaller and more aggressive because they have been infused with Pit Bull Terrier blood, but it *is* a curious coincidence.

It is more probable that these dogs have their common physical traits because the founders began their breeding programs with dogs that had inadvertently been bred from Pit Bull Terrier crosses. By selecting for certain physical and mental characteristics, they were merely breeding from the dogs which displayed these traits that they had inherited from their Pit Bull Terrier ancestors and no intentional cross breeding was done on their part. Most of these dogs are nice physical specimens, but they are just more aggressive than I think an American Bulldog should be.

Since the big-type American Bulldog is unquestionably the best man-stopping, family-oriented guard on the earth, I can't see any need to encourage it to be actively aggressive.

dogs they are referring to are dogs bred by John D. Johnson, or dogs bred from his bloodlines.

I've seen some of their dogs and they are very nice, as dogs. As American Bulldogs they tend to be noticeably smaller than most, much more aggressive towards other animals, and seem to show a remarkable tendency towards resembling a very large Pit Bull Terrier. The heads are often not as broad as I like to see and their muzzles often taper towards the nose in a triangular shape, much like a Pit Bull Terrier. Most, if not all, of the founders of this movement used to raise Pit Bull Terriers and still breed a few. This

The Standard for the American Bulldog

STANDARD OF PERFECTION FOR THE AMERICAN BULLDOG

General Appearance:

The American Bulldog is a powerful, athletic, heavyweight of a medium-large sized dog. Light on his feet, he moves with power and determination, giving the impression of speed, power, and agility. He is alert and inquisitive. He is bold and fearless without being hostile or overly aggressive. The first impression one should get is that of a very large, athletic Bulldog, not one of a powerful terrier.

Head:

The overall head is box-shaped. The skull should be large and square. The top of the skull is flat but covered with powerful muscles; there should be a distinct furrow between the eyes. There should be an abrupt, deep stop. The muzzle is also square and box-shaped. It should be deep, wide, and show power. The muzzle should be approximately 35 to 40 percent of the overall head length. Bite should be slightly (about one-eighth inch) undershot. Teeth large and powerful. The eyes should be round and set wide. Eyes should be brown. Ears may be either rose or flap, no preference. Ears may be carried semi-erect. Nose should have large, open nostrils and be black. *Faults:* A weak appearing or narrow head. Any noticeable tapering of the head to give a wedge-shaped appearance. Narrow or tapering muzzle. Excessively undershot to the point that the teeth are visible when the mouth is closed. Two blue eyes. Cropped ears. A pink or dudley nose not to be encouraged.

Without exaggeration, the head should be large overall and box-shaped.

The Standard for the American Bulldog

Body:

The body shall be robust and powerful. The American Bulldog is a broad, wide dog, but this width

The body of the American Bulldog should be broad and wide, giving the impression of power.

should not be exaggerated for the show ring. The chest should be deep with a good spring of ribs. The back is fairly short and very powerful. There should be a slight roach just over the loins, giving spring and power to the hindquarters. A level back is acceptable, but not preferred. Belly should be slightly tucked. The neck should match the body—fairly short, but not to the point of exaggeration, and thick and powerful. The neck is where the power of the dog is put to use against his opponent and it must

be long enough to apply leverage, short enough to exert power, and muscular enough to do the job. Shoulders shall be broad and heavily muscled. *Faults:* Any weakness or exaggeration. A weak, swayed back, or a back with a slope from the shoulders to the rump. The American Bulldog is a "working" Bulldog, and lack of power or agility are serious faults. Exaggeration of any part of the American Bulldog will reduce his effectiveness and ability to work and shall not be encouraged in the show ring.

Legs:

Front and rear legs shall be considered together because they must be balanced. The rear of the American Bulldog shall be heavily muscled, but it is not as broad as the shoulders. The rear legs shall be moderately angulated, and must be parallel. The front legs shall be straight and well muscled. *Faults:* Any semblance of weakness. Cow-hocks. A front whose feet turn either in or out. Some American Bulldogs can be so wide in the chest that the elbows appear to be pointing out when the dog is in motion, but if the front is correct the elbow will not point out when the dog is standing. Straight stifles or excessive angulation such as that seen in the German Shepherd Dog.

Tail:

The tail should be long enough to reach the hocks, or slightly past. It should be moderately thick and, as an extension of the spine, it should be powerful. The tail will often be carried above the back when the dog is moving or excited. It should end in a semi-circle, which is often evident when the dog carries it above his back.

Faults: A short tail, or a straight tail, showing no evidence of a curl at the end. The tail must not be docked.

Size:

The American Bulldog has been bred to work, not for the show ring; therefore, there is a wide size latitude in the breed. Males can be anywhere from 22 inches up to 28 inches at the shoulder. Bitches will be smaller, from about 17 inches up to 26 inches. Dogs should weigh from 90 pounds up to 135; bitches from 65 to 110 pounds. Weight shall be in proportion to the height: a 22-inch dog should weigh about 90 pounds, a 27- or 28-inch dog closer to 135. An ideal dog would probably be 25 inches at the shoulder and weigh 120 pounds. These weights are for well-muscled, conditioned dogs. The American Bulldog is a working dog and size alone is no criterion of quality. A well put together dog in hard condition at 110 pounds is preferable to an out-of-shape sloppy dog at 130 pounds, but a narrow, terrier-like dog is not typical of the breed and is to be discouraged. If all things

Blackwell's Ida Red is a nicely balanced bitch, a truly robust and spirited Bulldog.

are equal, the larger dog is preferred. *Faults:* Any deviation from the desired sizes, degree of fault according to the degree of deviation. Terrier-like dogs are to be avoided at all costs.

Color:

The preferred color is at least fifty percent white with patches of color. An all-white dog is equally acceptable but care must be taken to ascertain that there is no hearing problem with the all-white dog. The color patches may be any shade of brindle or any shade of brown (tan, red, yellow, fawn, etc.). A predominately colored dog with areas of white is next in order of preference (the same colors allowable), and then solid-colored dogs of these same colors. *Faults:* Solid black, black-and-tan, black-and-liver, merle, and fawn with black mask are not allowable. Fawn is acceptable if no mask is present.

Coat:

Short, hard, and shiny. The coat mirrors the dog's overall health and should be clean and bright.

Gait:

The American Bulldog should move with speed, agility, and power. There should be a definite spring in the step and the rear legs should propel the dog forward, not merely follow along behind. There should be definite stifle action in the rear legs. All legs should move parallel to the direction of travel. Front legs will not cross nor wing out to either side when the dog is in motion. Rear legs will not travel in an arc, but will move in a straight line in the direction of the dog's travel. Reach will be moderate, neither short and mincing nor approaching the reach of a Doberman Pinscher. *Faults:* Any deviation from the above.

DISQUALIFICATIONS:

Dogs under 75 pounds, bitches under 60 pounds. Black, black-and-tan, black-and-liver, merle, and fawn with a black mask. Dogs with less than two normal testicles. Cropped ears. Docked tails.

Note:

American Bulldogs whelped prior to January 1, 1990, may be shown with cropped ears and docked tails.

Scale of points:

General appearance	20
Size	15
Head	15
Body	15
Legs	10
Gait	10
Color	5
Tail	5
Coat	5
TOTAL	100

Selecting Your Dog

Now that you have decided which dog breed suits your needs, your lifestyle, and your own temperament, there will be much to consider before you make your final purchase. Buying a puppy on impulse may only cause heartbreak later on; it makes better sense to put some real thought into your canine investment, especially since it is likely that he will share many happy years with you. Which individual will you choose as your adoring companion? Ask yourself some questions as you analyze your needs and preferences for a dog, read all that you can about your particular breed, and visit as many dog shows as possible. At the shows you will be surrounded by people who can give you all the details about the breed that you are interested in buying. Decide if you want a household pet, a dog for breeding, or a show dog. Would you prefer a male or female? Puppy or adult?

Ask the seller to help you with your decision. When you have settled on the dog you want, discuss with the seller the dog's temperament, the animal's positive and negative aspects, any health problems it might have, its feeding and grooming requirements, and whether the dog has been immunized. Reputable sellers will be willing to answer any questions you

might have that pertain to the dog you have selected, and often they will make themselves available if you call for advice or if you encounter problems after you've made your purchase.

Dick the Cruiser and Kellen Symmes. The breed is respectful and affectionate with children.

33

A bit too big?
A little **too** small.
Too fuzzy for me!
Too fat to crawl.

Before you wrap it tight
And crate it home,
Behold its appetite
And room to roam.

A sloppy yap, a barking slur,
Puppy eyes to be let free,
A him? a her? an unmarked cur,
Let's pout to see its pedigree.

The perfect pet quest:
Which pup for me is best?

ANDREW DE PRISCO

35

Selecting Your Dog

Most breeders and sellers want to see their dogs placed in loving, responsible homes; they are careful about who buys their animals. So as the dog's new owner, prepare yourself for some interrogation from the from the person who sells you your pet.

WHERE TO BUY

You can choose among several places to buy your dog. Many people think of their local pet shop as the first source for buying a puppy, and very often they're right; you should

At ten weeks of age, this is Sugar. Puppies as wholesome as this little devil are bound to bring delight to a new owner.

remember, however, that a pet shop cannot possibly stock all breeds of dog. If your pet shop does not carry the type of dog you desire, there are other places to look. One is a kennel whose business is breeding show-quality dogs; such kennels may have extra pups for sale. Another source is the one-dog owner who wants to sell the puppies from an occasional litter to pay the expenses of his small-scale breeding operation. To find such kennels and part-time breeders and hobbyists, check the classified section of your local newspaper or look in your telephone directory.

Whichever source you choose, you can usually tell in a very short time whether the puppies will make healthy and happy pets. If they are clean, plump, and lively, they are probably in good health. Sometimes you will have the advantage of seeing the puppies' dam and perhaps their sire and other relatives. Remember that the mother, having just raised a demanding family, may not be looking her best; but if she is sturdy, friendly, and well-mannered, her puppies should be too. If you feel that something is lacking in the care or condition of the dogs, it is better to look elsewhere than to buy hastily and regret it afterward. Buy a healthy dog with a good disposition, one that has been properly socialized and

Blackwell's Champ at 125 pounds and friend Deborah. Properly trained, Bulldogs are great indoor companions.

likes being around people.

If you cannot find the dog you want locally, write to the secretary of the national breed club or kennel club and ask for names of breeders near you or to whom you can write for information. Puppies are sometimes shipped, sight unseen, from reputable breeders. In these instances, pictures and pedigree information are usually sent beforehand to help you decide.

Breeders can supply you with further details and helpful guidance, if you require it. Many breed clubs provide a puppy referral service, so you may want to look into this before making your final decision.

PET OR SHOW DOG

Conscientious breeders strive to maintain desirable qualities in their breed. At the same time, they are always working to improve on what they have already achieved, and they do this by referring to the breed standard of perfection. The standard describes the ideal dog, and those animals that come close to the ideal are generally selected as show

Owners of purebred dogs too often forget that all breeds of dog are interrelated. The ancient canine that is the believed ancestor of all dogs is known as Tomarctus. As packs traveled and inhabited various lands, types evolved through the process of adaptation. Later, as dogs and man joined forces, type became further diversified. This chart sketches one commonly accepted theory of the domesticated dog's development. Where does your dog fit in? With a few exceptions, dogs evolve or change as a result of a specific functional need.

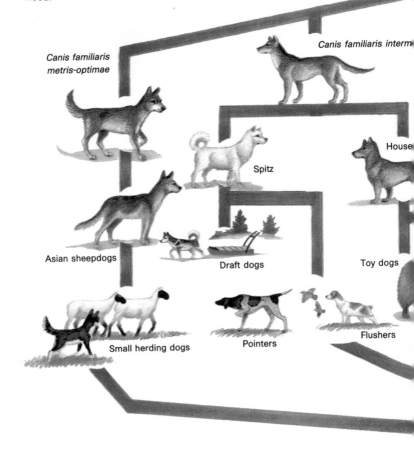

Canis familiaris metris-optimae

Canis familiaris interm

Spitz

House

Asian sheepdogs

Draft dogs

Toy dogs

Small herding dogs

Pointers

Flushers

Tomarctus

Canis familiaris leineri

Canis familiaris inostranzewi

Russian Tracker

Molossian

Scenthounds

Mastiffs

thound
otypes

Sighthounds

Terriers

Bulldogs

Retrievers

Large herding dogs

stock; those that do not are culled and sold as pets. Keep in mind that pet-quality purebred dogs are in no way less healthy or attractive than show-quality specimens. Sometimes these dogs even prove more hardy. It's just that the pet may have undesirable features (such as

Growing quickly, this is Blackwell's Preacher at just eight weeks of age. Can't wait to see how this puppy grows up!

ears that are too large or eyes that are the wrong color for the breed) which would be faults in the show ring. Often these so-called "flaws" are detectable only by experienced breeders or show judges. Naturally the more perfect animal, in terms of its breed standard, will cost more— even though he seems almost identical to his pet-quality littermate.

If you think you may eventually want to show your dog or raise a litter of puppies, by all means buy the best you can afford. You will save expense and disappointment later on. However, if the puppy is strictly to be a pet for the children, or a companion for you, you can afford to look for a bargain. The pup that is not show material, or the older pup for which there is often less demand, or the grown dog that is not being used for breeding is occasionally available and offers opportunities to save money. Remember that your initial investment may be a bargain, but it takes good food and care— and plenty of both—to raise a healthy, vigorous puppy through to adulthood.

__Facing Page:__ Kellen and Dick the Cruiser are inseparable companions. It's fair to say that Kellen has a competent babysitter.

The price you pay for your dog is little compared to the love and devotion he will return over the many years he'll be with you. With proper care and affection, your pup should live to a ripe old age; thanks to modern veterinary science and improvements in canine nutrition, dogs today are better maintained and live longer. It is not uncommon to see dogs living well into their teens.

Generally speaking, small dogs live longer than big ones. With love and the proper care any dog will live to its optimum age. Many persons, however, opt for a particular breed because of its proven longevity. This, of course, is purely a personal decision.

MALE OR FEMALE

Let us first disregard the usual generalizations and misconceptions applied to male vs. female dogs and consider the practical concerns. If you intend to show your new dog, a male will likely closer adhere to the

Size variation in the dog family is extreme. The consideration of size must be a high priority when choosing a breed. The amount of housing, exercise, and food required, as well as the animal's lifespan are just some of the factors involved.

breed standard, though ring competition for males is stiffer. A female chosen to show cannot be spayed and the owner must contend with the bitch's heat period. If it is solely a pet—and pet animals should *not* be bred—castration or spaying is necessary. Neutered pets have longer lifespans and have a decreased risk of cancer. Males are more economical to neuter than are females. You might also consider that females are generally smaller than males, easier to housetrain, may be more family-oriented and protective of home and property. Any dog will roam—male or female—castration will not affect roaming in most cases. Males are larger and stronger, proving better guard-dog candidates. Of course, a dog of either sex, if properly trained, can make a charming, reliable, and loving pet. Male vs. female is chiefly a matter of personal preference—go with your first instinct.

ADULT OR PUP

Whether to buy a grown dog or a young puppy is another question. It is surely an undeniable pleasure to watch your dog grow from a lively pup to a mature, dignified dog. If you don't have the time to spend on the more frequent meals, housebreaking, and other training a puppy needs in order to become a dog you can be

| Life Expectancy | |
Dog's Age in Years	Comparative Human Age in Years
1	15
2	24
3	28
4	32
5	36
6	40
7	44
8	48
9	52
10	56
11	60
12	64
13	68
14	72
15	76
16	80
17	84
18	88
19	92
20	96
21	100

This chart is designed to provide a comparative view of ages between a dog and its human counterpart. Necessarily it is an oversimplification since larger breeds often have shorter lifespans than do average or medium-sized dogs; likewise working dogs may tend to live shorter lives than the easygoing pet dog. These factors, and many others, must be taken into account when considering this chart.

proud of, then choose an older, partly trained adolescent or a grown dog. If you want a show dog, remember that no one, not even an expert, can predict with one hundred percent accuracy what a puppy will be like when he grows up. The dog may seem to exhibit show potential *most* of the time, but six months is the earliest age for the would-be exhibitor to select a prospect and know that its future is in the show ring.

If you have a small child, it is best to get a puppy big enough to defend itself, one not less than four or five months old.

Older children will enjoy playing with and helping to take care of a baby pup; but at less than four months, a puppy wants to do little else but eat and sleep, and he must be protected from teasing and overtiring. You cannot expect a very young child to understand that a puppy is a fragile living being; to the youngster he is a toy like his

Puppies of the American Bulldog breed are naturally loyal and devoted. Reinforcing these qualities begins with the breeder and assumed by the new owner.

A tough litter to pick from, out of Dozer and Ruby 1989.

stuffed dog. Children, therefore, must learn how to handle and care for their young pets.

We recommend that you start with a puppy so you can raise and train it according to the rules you have established in your own home. While a dog is young, its behavior can be more easily shaped by the owner, whereas an older dog, although trainable, may be a bit set in his ways.

WHAT TO LOOK FOR IN A PUPPY

In choosing a puppy, assuming that it comes from healthy, well-bred parents, look for one that is friendly and outgoing. The biggest pup in the litter is apt to be somewhat coarse as a grown dog, while the appealing "runt of the litter" may turn out to be a timid shadow—or have a Napoleonic complex! If you want a show dog and have no experience in choosing a prospect, study the breed standard and listen carefully to the breeder on the finer points of show conformation. A breeder's prices will be in accord with his puppies' expected worth, and he will be honest with you about each pup's potential because it is to his own advantage. He wants his top-quality show puppies placed in the public eye to reflect glory on him—and to attract future buyers. Why should he sell a potential show champion to someone who just wants a pet?

Now that you have paid your money and made your choice, you are ready to depart with puppy, papers, and instructions. Make sure that you know the youngster's feeding routine, and take along some of his food. For the trip home, place him in a comfortable, sturdy carrier. Do not drive home with a puppy on your lap! If you'll be travelling for a few hours, at the very least bring along a bottle of water from the breeder and a small water dish.

PEDIGREE AND REGISTRATION

Owners of puppies are often misled by sellers with such ruses as leading the owner to believe his dog is something special. The term *pedigree papers* is quite different from the term *registration papers*. A pedigree is nothing more than a statement made by the breeder of the dog;

If you have never been to a dog show, whether you're interested in show dogs or not, by all means—Go! An all-breed dog show will give you hands-on experience with different breeds of dog, the chance to meet their owners and breeders, and the answers to many of your questions.

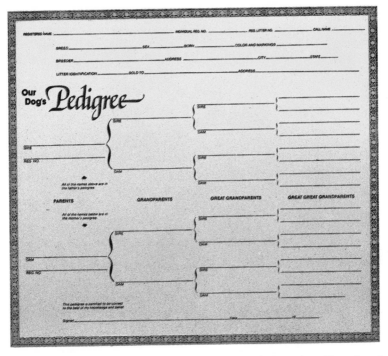

Pedigree papers can trace a dog's lineage back several generations. They do not, however, guarantee that a puppy is purebred, healthy or sound.

and it is written on special pedigree blanks, which are readily available from any pet shop or breed club, with the names of several generations from which the new puppy comes. It records your puppy's ancestry and other important data, such as the pup's date of birth, its breed, its sex, its sire and dam, its breeder's name and address, and so on. If your dog has had purebred champions in his background, then the pedigree papers are valuable as evidence of the good breeding behind your dog; but if the names on the pedigree paper are

meaningless, then so is the paper itself. Just because a dog has a pedigree doesn't necessarily mean he is registered with a kennel club.

Registration papers from the American Kennel Club or the United Kennel Club in the United States or The Kennel Club of Great Britain attest to the fact that the mother and father of your puppy were purebred dogs of the breed represented by your puppy and that they were registered with a particular club. Normally every registered dog also has a complete pedigree available. Registration papers, which you receive when you buy a puppy, merely enable you to register your puppy. Usually the breeder has registered only the litter, so it is the new owner's responsibility to register and name an individual pup. The papers should be filled out and sent to the appropriate address printed on the application, along with the fee required for the registration. A certificate of registration will then be sent to you.

Pedigree and registration, by the way, have nothing to do with licensing, which is a local regulation applying to purebred and mongrel alike. Find out what the local ordinance is in your town or city and how it applies to your dog; then buy a license and keep it on your dog's collar for identification.

As Rachael will concur, the young Ida Red is a good kisser. Bulldog pups love children especially—they are gentle and affectionate.

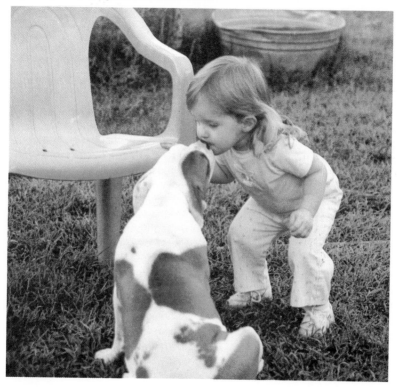

The New Family Member

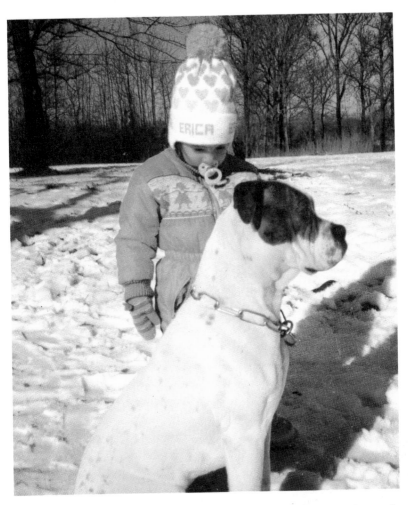

Bulldogs love to be a part of the family. Erica and her buddy are enjoying a wintertime outing.

At long last, the day you have all been waiting for, your new puppy will make its grand entrance into your home. Before you bring your companion to his new residence, however, you must plan carefully for his arrival. Keep in mind that the puppy will need

The New Family Member

time to adjust to life with a different owner. He may seem a bit apprehensive about the strange surroundings in which he finds himself, having spent the first few weeks of life with his dam and littermates, but in a couple of days, with love and patience on your part, the transition will be complete.

First impressions are important, especially from the puppy's point of view, and these may very well set the pattern of his future relationship with you. You must be consistent in the

The puppy's bed will provide a place of refuge and privacy. Make sure that the puppy's toilet needs have been met before sending him to bed for the night.

way you handle your pet so that he learns what is expected of him. He must come to trust and respect you as his keeper and master. Provide him with proper care and attention, and you will be rewarded with a loyal companion for many years. Considering the needs of your puppy and planning ahead will surely make the change from his former home to his new one easier.

ADVANCE PREPARATION

In preparing for your puppy's arrival, perhaps more important than anything else is to find out from the seller how the pup was maintained. What brand of food was offered and when and how often was the puppy fed? Has

BASIC PUPPY NEEDS

- Canned and dry food/diet schedule
- Feeding and water bowls
- Carrying/sleeping crate
- Bed
- Collar and leash
- Grooming supplies (brushes, shampoo, etc.)
- Outdoor lead and/or pen
- Muzzle/first-aid kit
- Flea collar and preparations
- Safe chew products (Nylabone®, Gumabone®)
- Edible chew products (treats/rewards)

the pup been housebroken; if so, what method was employed? Attempt to continue whatever routine was started by the person from whom you bought your puppy; then, gradually, you can make those changes that suit you and your lifestyle. If, for example, the puppy has been paper trained, plan to stock up on newspaper. Place this newspaper toilet facility in a selected spot so that your puppy learns to use the designated area as his "bathroom." And keep on hand a supply of the dog food to which he is accustomed, as a sudden switch to new food could cause digestive upsets.

Another consideration is sleeping and resting quarters. Be sure to supply a dog bed for your pup, and introduce him to his special cozy corner so that he

This chart lists some of the many items that the dog owner should have on hand before he brings home his new charge.

knows where to retire when he feels like taking a snooze. You'll need to buy a collar (or harness) and leash, a safe chew item (such as Nylabone® or Gumabone®), and a few grooming tools as well. A couple of sturdy feeding dishes, one for food and one for water, will be needed; and it will be necessary, beforehand, to set up a feeding station.

FINDING A VETERINARIAN

An important part of your preparations should include finding a local veterinarian who can provide quality health care in the form of routine check-ups, inoculations, and prompt medical attention in case of illness or emergency. Find out if the animal you have selected has been vaccinated against canine diseases, and make certain you secure all health certificates at the time of purchase. This information will be valuable to your veterinarian, who will want to know the puppy's complete medical history. Incidentally, don't wait until your puppy becomes sick before you seek the services of a vet; make an appointment for your pup before or soon after he takes up residence with you so that he starts out with a clean bill of health in his new home.

CHILDREN AND PUPPIES

Instruct the young members of the household on pet care. Children should learn not only to love their charges but to respect them and treat them with the consideration that one would give all living things. It must be emphasized to youngsters that the puppy has certain needs, just as humans have, and all family members must take an active role in ensuring that these needs are met. Someone must feed the puppy. Someone must walk him a couple of times a day or clean up after him if he is trained to relieve himself on newspaper. Someone must groom his coat, clean his ears, and clip his nails from time to time. Someone,

must see to it that the puppy gets sufficient exercise and attention each day.

A child who has a pet to care for learns responsibility; nonetheless, parental guidance is an essential part of this learning experience. Many a child has been known to "love a pet to death," squeezing and hugging the animal in ways which are irritating or even painful. Others have been found guilty of teasing, perhaps unintentionally, and disturbing their pet while the animal is eating or resting. One must teach a child, therefore, when and how to stroke and fondle a puppy gently. In time, the child can learn how to pick up and handle the pup with care. A dog should always be supported with both hands, *not* lifted by the scruff of the neck. One hand placed under the chest, between the front legs, and the other hand supporting the dog's rear end will be comfortable and will restrain the animal as you hold and carry it. Always demonstrate to children the proper way to lift a dog.

BE A GOOD NEIGHBOR

For the sake of your dog's safety and well being, don't allow him to wander onto the property of others. Keep him confined at all times to your own yard or indoors where he won't become a nuisance. Consider what

The expression of the American Bulldog, with its cocked head and soulful eyes, is genuine and all-American.

Clockwise from upper right: *pokeweed, jimson weed, foxglove, and yew.* If ingested, any toxic plant can be dangerous to your dog.

ROVER WILL NOT BE HARMED IF YOU FOLLOW MY INSTRUCTIONS

AMF

Dog theft is not an uncommon event. Dognappers will steal either a purebred or mongrel puppy so all owners must always be wary.

dangers lie ahead for an unleashed dog that has total freedom of the great outdoors, particularly when he is unsupervised by his master. There are cars and trucks to dodge on the streets and highways. There are stray animals with which to wrangle. There are poisons all around, such as car antifreeze in driveways or toxic plants and shrubs, which, if swallowed, could prove fatal. There are dognappers and sadistic people who may steal or bring harm to your beloved pet. In short, there are all sorts of nasty things waiting to hurt him. Did you know that if your dog consumes rotting garbage, there is the possibility he could go into shock or even die? And are you aware that a dog left to roam in a wooded area or field could become infected with any number of parasites if he plays with or ingests some small prey, such as a rabbit, that might be carrying these parasitic organisms? A thorn from a rosebush imbedded in the dog's foot pad, tar from a newly paved road stuck to his coat, and a wound inflicted by a wild animal all can be avoided if you take the precaution of keeping your dog in a safe enclosure where he will be protected from such dangers. Don't let your dog run loose; he is likely to stray from home and get into all sorts of trouble.

The New Family Member

GETTING ACQUAINTED

Plan to bring your new pet home in the morning so that by nightfall he will have had some time to become acquainted with you and his new environment. Avoid introducing the pup to the family around holiday time, since the extra excitement will only add to the confusion and frighten him. Let the puppy enter your home on a day when the routine

Resist the temptation to handle him too much during these first few days. And, if there are other dogs or animals around the house, make certain that all are properly introduced. If you observe fighting among the animals, or some other problem, you may have to separate all parties until they learn to accept one another. Remember that neglecting your other pets while

is normal. For those people who work during the week, a Saturday morning is an ideal time to bring the puppy to his new home. Let the puppy explore, under your watchful eye, of course, and let him come to know his new home without stress and fear.

Bulldogs are generally good with other pets if properly introduced; likely the family Manx will define its own space.

Facing Page: *Johnson's Dick the Bruiser and Johnson's Sugar Tuffy enjoy the benefits of a smart kennel set-up.*

showering the new puppy with extra attention will only cause animosity and jealousy. Make an effort to pay special attention to the other animals as well.

On that eventful first night, try not to give in and let the puppy sleep with you; otherwise, this could become a difficult habit to break. Let him cry and whimper, even if it means a night of restlessness for the entire family. Some people have had success with putting a doll or a hot water bottle wrapped in a towel in the puppy's bed as a surrogate mother, while others have placed a ticking alarm clock in the bed to simulate the heartbeat of the pup's dam and littermates. Remember that this furry little fellow is used to the warmth and security of his mother and siblings, so the adjustment to sleeping alone will take time. Select a location away from drafts and away from the feeding station for placement of his dog bed. Keep in mind, also, that the bed should be roomy enough for him to stretch out in; as he grows older, you may need to supply a larger one.

Prior to the pup's arrival, set up his room and partition it the way you would to keep an infant out of a particular area. You may want to keep his bed, his feeding station, and his toilet area all in the same room—in separate locations—or you may want to set the feeding station up in your kitchen, where meals for all family members are served. Whatever you decide, do it ahead of time so you will have that much less to worry about when your puppy finally moves in with you.

Above all else, be patient with your puppy as he adjusts to life in his new home. If you purchase a pup that is not housebroken, you will have to spend time with the dog—just as you would with a small child—until he develops proper toilet habits. Even a housebroken puppy may feel nervous in strange new surroundings and have an occasional accident. Praise and encouragement will elicit far better results than punishment or scolding. Remember that your puppy wants nothing more than to please you, thus he is anxious to learn the behavior that is required of him.

Feeding Requirements

Perhaps more than any other single aspect of your dog's development, proper feeding requires an educated and responsible dog owner. The importance of nutrition on your dog's bone and muscle growth cannot be overemphasized.

Soon after your puppy comes to live with you, he will need to be fed. Remember to ask the seller what foods were given to the youngster and stay with that diet for a while. It is important for the puppy to keep eating and to avoid skipping a meal, so entice him with the food to which he is accustomed. If you prefer to switch to some other brand of dog food, each day begin to add small quantities of the new brand to the usual food offering. Make the portions of the new food progressively larger until the pup is weaned from his former diet.

What should you feed the puppy and how often? His diet is really quite simple and relatively inexpensive to prepare. Puppies need to be fed small portions at frequent intervals, since they are growing and their activity level is high. You must ensure that your pup gains weight steadily; with an adult dog, however, growth slows down and weight must be regulated to prevent obesity and a host of other problems. At one time, it was thought that home-cooked meals were the answer, with daily rations of meat,

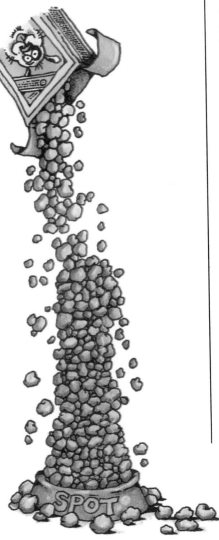

Choosing a quality dog food from your pet shop is easy—deciding how much to feed may not be as straightforward. Feedings must always be carefully monitored.

vegetables, egg yolk, cereal, cheese, brewer's yeast, and vitamin supplements. With all of the nutritionally complete commercial dog food products readily available, these time-consuming preparations really are unnecessary now. A great deal of money and research has resulted in foods that we can serve our dogs with confidence and pride; and most of these commercial foods have been developed along strict guidelines according to the size, weight, and age of your dog. These products are reasonably priced,

At 115 pounds, the well-nourished Rip N' Woody excels as a family dog and a wild boar hunter. Owner, Kyle Symmes.

easy to find, and convenient to store.

THE PUPPY'S MEALS

After a puppy has been fully weaned from its mother until approximately three months of age, it needs to be fed four times a day. In the morning and evening, offer kibble (dog meal) soaked in hot water or broth, to which you have added some canned meat-based food or fresh raw meat cut into small chunks. At noon and bedtime feed him a bit of kibble or whole-grain cereal moistened with milk (moistening, by the way, makes the food easier to digest, since dogs don't typically chew their food). From three to six months, increase the portion size and offer just three meals—one milk

Suzie with Dozer Bruno . . . at 125 pounds, Dozer is a "serious" protector. Owner, David Farnetti of Vestal, NY.

and two meat. At six months, two meals are sufficient; at one year, a single meal can be given, supplemented with a few dry biscuits in the morning and evening. During the colder months, especially if your dog is active, you might want to mix in some wheat germ oil or corn oil or meat drippings with the meal to add extra calories. Remember to keep a bowl of cool, fresh water always on hand to help your dog regulate his body temperature and to aid in digestion.

From one year on, you may continue feeding the mature dog a single meal (in the evening, perhaps, when you have your supper), or you may prefer to divide this meal in two, offering half in the morning and the other half at night. Keep in mind that while puppies require foods in small chunks or nuggets, older dogs can handle larger pieces of food at mealtime. Discuss your dog's feeding schedule with your veterinarian; he can make suggestions about the right diet for your particular canine friend.

COMPARISON SHOPPING

With so many fine dog-food products on the market today, there is something for

Feeding Requirements

everyone's pet. You may want to serve dry food "as is" or mix it with warm water or broth. Perhaps you'll choose to combine dry food with fresh or canned preparations. Some canned foods contain all meat, but they are not complete; others are mixtures of meat and grains, which have been fortified with additional nutrients to make them more complete and balanced. There are also various packaged foods that can be served alone or as supplements and that can be left out for a few hours without spoiling. This self-feeding method, which works well for dogs that are not prone to weight problems, allows the animal to serve himself whenever he feels hungry. Many people who work during the day find these dry or semi-moist rations convenient to use, and these foods are great to bring along if you travel with your dog.

Be sure to read the labels carefully before you make your dog-food purchases. Most

Feeder bins are used by many kennel owners as well as pet owners. These devices help to conveniently store and distribute dry foods in a sanitary, efficient way.

Pet shops offer a variety of dry kibbles. Though the nutritional values of these foods are essentially equivalent, compare the manufacturer's labels.

reputable pet-food manufacturers list the ingredients and the nutritional content right on the can or package. Instructions are usually included so that you will know how much to feed your dog to keep him thriving and in top condition. A varied, well-balanced diet that supplies the proper amounts of protein, carbohydrate, fat, vitamins, minerals, and water is important to keep your puppy healthy and to guarantee his normal development. Adjustments to the diet can be made, under your veterinarian's supervision, according to the individual puppy, his rate of growth, his activity level, and so on. Liquid or powder vitamin and mineral supplements, or those in tablet form, are available and can be given if you need to feel certain that the diet is balanced.

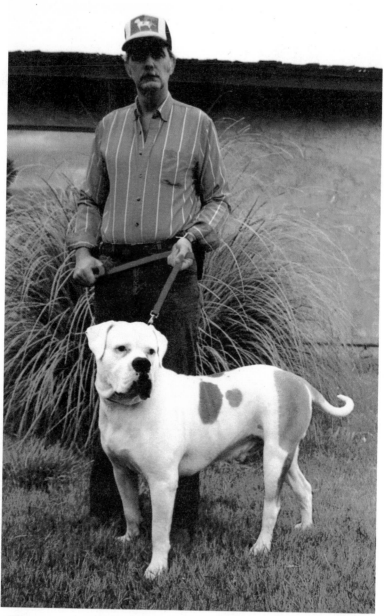

Joel Thompson with the handsome and imposing Blackwell's Champ. He weighs in at 125 pounds and is surely a fine dog.

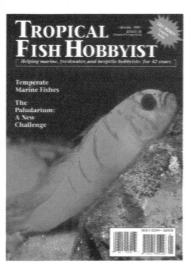

Since 1952, *Tropical Fish Hobbyist* has been the source of accurate, up-to-the-minute, and fascinating information on every facet of the aquarium hobby. Join the more than 50,000 devoted readers world-wide who wouldn't miss a single issue.

Subscribe right now so you don't miss a single copy!

DEVELOPING GOOD EATING HABITS

Try to serve your puppy his meals at the same time each day and in the same location so that he will get used to his daily routine and develop good eating habits. A bit of raw egg, cottage cheese, or table scraps (leftover food from your own meals) can

Feeding your dog is made easy by the use of sturdy non-tip, easy-clean bowls. Pet shops offer the best selection of colors, styles and sizes.

be offered from time to time; but never accustom your dog to eating human "junk food." Cake, candy, chocolate, soda, and other snack foods are for people, not dogs. Besides, these foods provide only "empty" calories that your pet doesn't need if he is to stay healthy. Avoid offering spicy, fried, fatty, or starchy foods; rather, offer leftover meats, vegetables, and gravies. Get in the habit of feeding your puppy or your grown dog his *own* daily meals of dog food. If ever you are in doubt about what foods and how much to serve, consult your veterinarian.

Feeding Requirements

FEEDING GUIDELINES

Some things to bear in mind with regard to your dog's feeding regimen follow.

- Nutritional balance, provided by many commercial dog foods, is vital; avoid feeding a one-sided all-meat diet. Variety in the kinds of meat (beef, lamb, chicken, liver) or cereal grains (wheat, oats, corn) that

Automatic feeders are handy modern devices, available from most good pet shops. Overfeeding can be a drawback of this method of feeding.

you offer your dog is of secondary importance compared to the balance or "completeness" of dietary components.

- Always refrigerate opened canned food so that it doesn't spoil. Remember to remove all uneaten portions of canned or moistened food from the feeding dish as soon as the pup has finished his meal. Discard the leftover food immediately and thoroughly wash and dry the feeding dish, as a dirty dish is a breeding ground for harmful germs.

- When offering dry foods, always keep a supply of water on hand for your dog. Water should be made available at all times, even if dry foods are not left out for self-feeding. Each day the water dish should be washed with soap and hot water, rinsed well, and dried; a refill of clean, fresh water should be provided daily.

- Food and water should be served at room temperature, neither too hot nor too cold, so that it is more palatable for your puppy.

- Serve your pup's meals in sturdy hard-plastic, stainless steel, or earthenware containers, ones that won't tip over as the dog gulps his food down. Some bowls and dishes are weighted to prevent spillage, while others fit neatly into holders which offer support. Feeding dishes should be large enough to hold each meal.

- Whenever the nutritional needs of your dog change—that is to say, when it grows older or if it becomes ill, obese, or pregnant; or if it starts to nurse its young—special diets are in order. Always contact your vet for advice on these special dietary requirements.

- Hard foods, such as biscuits and dog meal, should be offered regularly. Chewing on these hard, dry morsels helps the dog keep its teeth clean and its gums conditioned.

- Never overfeed your dog. If given the chance, he will accept and relish every in-between-meal tidbit you offer him. This pampering will only put extra weight on your pet and cause him to be unhealthy.

New treats on the block by Chooz®. These crunchy dog bones are delectable and affordable.

- Feed your puppy at the same regular intervals each day; reserve treats for special occasions or, perhaps, to reward good behavior.

- Do not encourage your dog to beg for food from the table while you are eating your meals.

- Food can be effectively used by the owner to train the dog. Doggie treats are practical and often nutritional—choose your chew treats choosily.

FEEDING CHART

Age and No. of Feedings Per Day	Weight in Lbs.	Weight in Kg.	Caloric Requirement kcal M.E./Day
Puppies—Weaning to 3 months Four per day	1–3 3–6 6–12 12–20 15–30	.5–1.4 1.4–2.7 2.7–5.4 5.4–9.1 6.8–13.6	124–334 334–574 574–943 943–1384 1113–1872
Puppies—3 to 6 months Three per day	3–10 5–15 12–25 20–40 30–70	1.4–4.5 2.3–6.8 5.4–11.3 9.1–18.2 13.6–31.8	334–816 494–1113 943–1645 1384–2352 1872–3542
Puppies—6 to 12 months Two per day	6–12 12–25 20–50 40–70 70–100	2.7–5.4 5.4–11.3 9.1–22.7 18.2–31.8 31.8–45.4	574–943 943–1645 1384–2750 2352–3542 3542–4640
Normally Active Adults One or two per day	6–12 12–25 25–50 50–90 90–175	2.7–5.4 5.4–11.3 11.3–22.7 22.7–40.8 40.8–79.4	286–472 472–823 823–1375 1375–2151 2151–3675

This chart presents general parameters of the dog's caloric requirements, based on weight. The total caloric intake comes from a complete, balanced diet of quality foods. To assist owners, dog food companies generally provide the nutritional information to their product right on the label.

Accommodations

Puppies newly weaned from their mother and siblings should be kept warm at all times. As they get older, they can be acclimated gradually to cooler temperatures. When you purchase your dog, find out from the seller whether he is hardy and can withstand the rigors of outdoor living. Many breeds have been known to adapt well to a surprising number of environments, so long as they are given time to adjust. If your pup is to be an indoor for your pooch; or you may find that a heated garage or finished basement works well as your dog's living quarters. If your breed can tolerate living outside, you may want to buy or build him his own dog house with an attached run. It might be feasible to place his house in your fenced-in backyard. The breed that can live outdoors fares well when given access to some sort of warm, dry shelter during periods of inclement weather. As you begin thinking about where

companion, perhaps a dog bed in the corner of the family room will suffice; or you may want to invest in a crate for him to call his "home" whenever he needs to be confined for short intervals. You might plan to partition off a special room, or part of a room,

A bed for your dog gives him a place to call his own. His bed should be placed in a warm, dry, draft-free area.

Accommodations

your canine friend will spend most of his time, you'll want to consider his breed, his age, his temperament, his need for exercise, and the money, space, and resources you have available to house him.

your puppy something with which to snuggle, such as a laundered towel or blanket or an article of old clothing. Some dogs have been known to chew apart their beds and bedding, but you can easily channel this

THE DOG BED

In preparing for your puppy's arrival, it is recommended that a dog bed be waiting for him so that he has a place to sleep and rest. If you have provided him with his own bed or basket, ensure that it is placed in a warm, dry, draft-free spot that is private but at the same time near the center of family activity. Refrain from placing his bed near the feed and water dishes or his toilet area. You may want to give

Beds can have personality. Pet shops offer many different bedding options to the owner willing to explore.

chewing energy into more constructive behavior simply by supplying him with some safe toys or a Nylabone® pacifier for gnawing. Pet shops stock dog beds, among other supplies that you might need for your pup. Select a bed that is roomy, comfortable, and easy to clean, keeping in mind that you may have to replace the smaller bed with a larger one as the puppy grows to adulthood. Remember to clean and disinfect the bed and sleeping area from time to time, as these can become parasitic playgrounds for fleas, lice, mites, and the like.

THE CRATE

Although many dog lovers may cringe at the mere mention of the word *crate,* thinking of it as a cage or a cruel means of confinement, this handy piece of equipment can be put to good use for puppies and grown dogs alike. Even though you may love your dog to an extraordinary degree, you may not want him to have free reign of the house, particularly when you are not home to supervise him. If used properly, a crate can restrict your dog when it is not convenient to have him underfoot, *i.e.,* when guests are visiting or during your mealtimes.

A surprising number of dog owners, who originally had negative feelings about crating their dogs, have had great success using crates. The crate itself serves as a bed, provided it is furnished with bedding material, or it can be used as an indoor dog house. Not all dogs

The wire crate is a most effective means to accelerate housebreaking and is the safest way to ensure that the puppy is safe when he cannot be supervised.

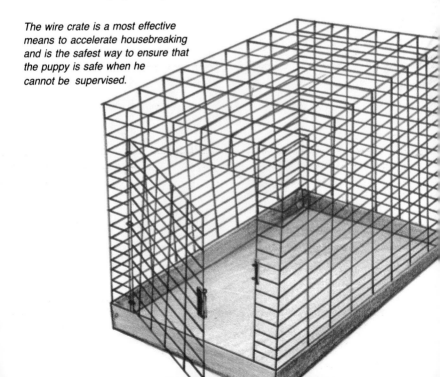

readily accept crates or being confined in them for short intervals, so for these dogs, another means of restriction must be found. But for those dogs that do adjust to spending time in these structures, the crate can be useful in many ways. The animal can be confined for a few hours while you are away from home or at work, or you can bring your

If your living arrangement allows, an outdoor run connected to the house by a swinging pet door can provide an ideal accommodation for your dog.

crated dog along with you in the car when you travel or go on vacation. Crates also prove handy as carriers whenever you have to transport a sick dog to the veterinarian.

Most crates are made of sturdy wire or plastic, and some of the collapsible models can be conveniently stored or folded so that they can be moved easily from room to room or from inside the house to the yard on a warm, sunny day. If you allow your puppy or grown dog to become acquainted with its crate by cleverly propping the door open and leaving some of his favorite toys inside, in no time he will come to regard the crate as his own doggie haven. As with a dog bed, place the crate away from drafts in a dry, warm spot; refrain from placing food and water dishes in it, as these only crowd the space and offer opportunity for spillage.

If you need to confine your puppy so that he can't get into mischief while you're not home, remember to consider the animal's needs at all times. Select a large crate, one in which the dog can stand up and move around comfortably; in fact, bigger is better in this context. Never leave the animal confined for more than a few hours at a time without letting him out to exercise, play, and, if necessary, relieve himself. Never crate a dog for ten hours, for example, unless you keep the door to the crate open so that he can get out for food and water and to stretch a bit. If long intervals of confinement are necessary, consider placing the unlatched crate in a partitioned section of your house or apartment.

Crates have become the answer for many a dog owner faced with the dilemma of either getting rid of a destructive dog or living with him despite his bad habits. People who have neither the time nor the patience to train their dogs, or to modify undesirable behavior patterns, can at least restrain their pets during the times they can't be

Traveling crates can provide safe and easy transport for your dog. Ventilation for travel is a most important consideration.

there to supervise. So long as the crate is used in a humane fashion, whereby a dog is confined for no more than a few hours at any one time, it can figure importantly in a dog owner's life. Show dogs,

The pet trade offers many commercially made dog houses and other outdoor living structures that make great temporary accommodations for your pet.

incidentally, learn at an early age that much time will be spent in and out of crates while they are on the show circuit. Many canine celebrities are kept in their crates until they are called to ringside, and they spend many hours crated to and from the shows.

THE DOG HOUSE

These structures, often made of wood, should be sturdy and offer enough room for your dog to stretch out in when it rests or sleeps. Dog houses that are elevated or situated on a platform protect the animal from cold and dampness that may seep through the ground. For the breeds that are temperature hardy and will live outdoors, a dog house is an excellent option for daytime occupancy. Owners who cannot provide indoor accommodations for their chosen dog should consider a smaller breed since no dog should lead an exclusively outdoor existence.

If you have no option but to accommodate your dog with only an outdoor house, it will be necessary to provide him with a more elaborate house, one that really protects him from the elements. Make sure the dog's house is constructed of waterproof materials. Furnish him with sufficient bedding to burrow into on a chilly night and provide extra insulation to keep

out drafts and wet weather. Add a partition (a kind of room divider which separates the entry area from the main sleeping space) inside his house or attach a swinging door to the entrance to help keep him warm when he is inside his residence. The

Indoor-outdoor dog houses offer pest-free, sanitary conditions for your dog. These attractive living options can be acquired from pet shops, supply outlets or mail-order catalogues.

swinging door facilitates entry to and from the dog house, while at the same time it provides protection, particularly from wind and drafts.

Some fortunate owners whose yards are enclosed by high freedom is a dog kennel or run which attaches to or surrounds the dog's house. This restricts some forms of movement, such as running, perhaps, but it does provide ample room for walking, climbing, jumping, and

An anchored lead can provide efficient temporary restraint. This is not a viable substitute for a fenced-in yard and no dog should be left unsupervised on such a lead for any length of time.

fencing allow their dogs complete freedom within the boundaries of their property. In these situations, a dog can leave his dog house and get all the exercise he wants. Of course such a large space requires more effort to keep it clean. An alternative to complete backyard stretching. Another option is to fence off part of the yard and place the dog house in the enclosure. If you need to tether your dog to its house, make certain to use a fairly long lead so as not to hamper the animal's need to move and exercise his limbs.

CLEANLINESS

No matter where your dog lives, either in or out of your home, be sure to keep him in surroundings that are as clean and sanitary as possible. His excrement should be removed and disposed of every day without fail. No dog should be forced to lie in his own feces. If your dog lives in his own house, the floor should be swept occasionally and the bedding should be changed regularly if it becomes soiled. Food and water dishes need to be scrubbed with hot water and detergent and rinsed well to remove all traces of soap. The water dish should be refilled with a supply of fresh water. The dog and his environment must be kept free of parasites (especially fleas and mosquitoes, which can carry disease) with products designed to keep these pests under control. Dog crates need frequent scrubbing, too, as do the floors of kennels and runs. Your pet must be kept clean and comfortable at all times; if you exercise strict sanitary control, you will keep disease and parasite infestation to a minimum.

EXERCISE

A well-balanced diet and regular medical attention from a qualified veterinarian are essential in promoting good health for your dog, but so is

Most cities and towns require dog owners to clean up after their pets. Commercial pooper scoopers can make curbing your dog more convenient and sanitary.

daily exercise to keep him fit and mentally alert. Dogs that have been confined all day while their owners are at work or school need special attention. There should be some time set aside each day for play—a romp with a family member, perhaps. Not everyone is lucky enough to let his dog run through an open meadow or along a sandy beach, but even a ten-minute walk in the fresh air will do Dogs that are house-bound, particularly those that live in apartments, need to

Flying discs are popular with most dog owners, child and adult alike. Many dogs display a natural talent for Frisbee® games.

be walked out-of-doors after each meal so that they can relieve themselves. Owners can make this daily ritual more pleasant both for themselves

and their canine companions by combining the walk with a little "roughhousing," that is to say, a bit of fun and togetherness.

Whenever possible, take a stroll to an empty lot, a playground, or a nearby park. Attach a long lead to your dog's collar, and let him run and jump and tone his body through aerobic activity. This will help him burn calories and will keep him trim, and it will also help relieve tension and stress that may have had a chance to develop while you were away all day. For people who work Monday through Friday, weekend jaunts can be especially beneficial, since there will be more time to spend with your canine friend. You might want to engage him in a simple game of fetch with a stick or a rubber ball. Even such basic tricks as rolling over, standing on

by all means do it. Don't neglect your pet and leave him confined for long periods without attention from you or time for exercise.

the hindlegs, or jumping up (all of which can be done inside the home as well) can provide additional exercise. But if you plan to challenge your dog with a real workout to raise his heart rate, remember not to push him too hard without first warming up with a brisk walk. Don't forget to "cool him down" afterwards with a rhythmic trot until his heart rate returns to normal. Some dog owners jog with their dogs or take them along on bicycle excursions.

At the very least, however, play with your dog every day to keep him in good shape physically and mentally. If you can walk him outdoors, or better yet run with him in a more vigorous activity,

Fitness and exercise are on the move. Getting in on the trim-and-active side ain't just a doggie obsession—owners should sneak in too!

EXERCISING FOR YOU AND YOUR DOG

Dogs are like people. They come in three weights: overweight, underweight, and the correct weight. It is fair to say that most dogs are in better shape than most humans who own them. The reason for this is that most dogs accept exercise without objection—people do not! Follow your dog's lead towards exercise and the complete enjoyment of the outdoors—your dog is the ideal work-out partner. There are toys

79

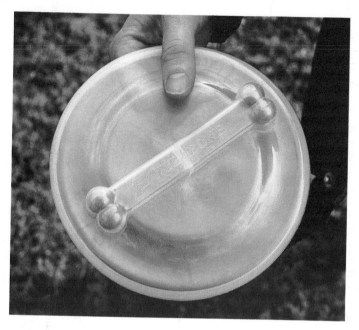

at your local pet shop which are designed just for that purpose: to allow you to play and exercise with your dog. Here are a few recommended exercise toys for you and your dog.

Frisbee® Flying Discs Most dog owners capitalize on the dog's natural instinct to fetch or retrieve, and the Frisbee® flying disc is standard fare for play. The original Frisbee® is composed of polyethylene plastic, ideal for flying and great for games of catch between two humans. Since humans don't usually chew on their flying discs, there is no need for a "chew-worthy" construction material. Dogs, on the other

The most popular in flying discs designed especially for dogs is the Nylabone Frisbee®, a toy that outlasts plastic discs by ten times. The molded dog bone on the top makes for easy retrieves by your dog.

hand, do chew on their Frisbees® and therefore should not be allowed to play with a standard original Frisbee®. These discs will be destroyed quickly by the dog and the rigid plastic can cause intestinal complications.

Nylon Discs More suitable for playing with dogs are the Frisbee® discs that are constructed from nylon. These durable Frisbee® discs are designed especially for dogs and the nearly indestructible manufacturing makes them ideal for aggressive chewing dogs. For play with dogs, the nylon discs called Nylabone Frisbee® are guaranteed to last ten times as long as the regular plastic Frisbee®. Owners should carefully consider the size of the nylon Frisbee® they purchase. A rule of thumb is choose the largest disc that your dog can comfortably carry. Nylabone manufactures two sizes only—toy and large—so the choice should be apparent.

Polyurethane Flexible Floppy Flying Discs The greatest advance in flying discs came with the manufacture of these discs from polyurethane. The polyurethane is so soft that it doesn't hurt you, your dog, or the window it might strike accidentally. The polyurethane Gumadisc® is floppy and soft. It can be folded and fits into your pocket. It is also much tougher than cheap plastics, and most pet shops guarantee that it will last ten times longer than cheap plastic discs.

Making the polyurethane discs even more suited to dog play is the fact that many of the Gumabone® Frisbee® Flexible Fly Discs have the advantage of a dog bone molded on the top. Very often a Frisbee® without the bone molded on the top is difficult for a dog to pick up

Made of durable and flexible polyurethane, the Gumabone Frisbees® prove chew-worthy and good-smelling to dogs. These and other Nylabone® discs are available in pet shops and other stores.

*Frisbee® is a trademark of the Kransco Company, California, and is used for their brand of flying disc.

when it lands on a flat surface. The molded ones enable the dog to grasp it with his mouth or turn it with his paw. Dogs love pawing at the bone and even chew on it occasionally.

This product has one further capacity—it doubles as a temporary drinking dish while out running, hiking and playing. The Gumabone Frisbee® flyers may also be flavored or scented, besides being annealed, so your dog can find it more easily if it should get lost in woods or tall grass.

with your canine friend. Basically, you play with the dog and the disc so the dog knows the disc belongs to him. Then you throw it continuously,

Toys made for doggie tug-of-wars are popular with lots of pet owners. These tug toys are durable and last a long time.

Flying discs manufactured by the Nylabone® Company may cost more than some of its imitators, but an owner can be assured that the product will last and not be quickly destroyed.

With most flying discs made for dogs comes an instruction booklet on how to use the disc

increasing the distance, so that the dog fetches it and brings it back to you.

The exercise for you comes in when your dog stops fetching it, or when you have a partner. The two of you play catch. You stand as far apart as available space allows—usually 30–35 m (100

Great for the athletic dog and less-active owner are commercially designed retractable leads which give the dog much freedom when exercising in an open field or cleared area.

feet) is more than enough room. You throw the disc to each other, arousing your dog's interest as he tries to catch it. When the disc is dropped or veers off, the dog grabs it and brings it back (hopefully). Obviously you will have to run to catch the disc before your dog does.

There are contests held all over the world where distance, height, and other characteristics are measured competitively. Ask your local pet shop to help you locate a Frisbee® Club near you.

Tug Toys A tug toy is a hard rubber, cheap plastic, or polyurethane toy which allows a

*Frisbee® is a trademark of the Kransco Company, California, and is used for their brand of flying disc.

The more consideration given to the canine's needs, the better the outdoor accommodations will be. Owners planning an outdoor kennel set-up must consider the elements (sun, rain, and wind) as well as sanitation and security.

dog and his owner to have a game of tug-o-war. The owner grips one end while the dog grips the other—then they pull. The polyurethane flexible tug toy is the best on the market at the present time. Your pet shop will have one to show you. The polyurethane toys are clear in color and stay soft forever. Cheap plastic tug toys are indisputably dangerous, and the hard-rubber tug toys get brittle too fast and are too stiff for most dogs; however, there *is* a difference in price—just ask the advice of any pet shop operator.

Balls Nobody has to tell you about playing ball with your dog. The reminder you may need is that you should not throw the ball where traffic might interfere with the dog's catching or fetching of it. The ball should not be cheap plastic (a dog's worst enemy as far as toys are concerned) but made of a substantial material. Balls made of nylon are practically indestructible, but they are very hard and must be rolled, never thrown. The same balls made of polyurethane are great—they bounce and are soft. The Nylaballs® and Gumaballs® are scented and flavored, and dogs can easily find them when lost.

Other manufacturers make balls of almost every substance, including plastic, cotton, and wood. Soft balls, baseballs, tennis balls, and so on, have all been used by dog owners who want their dogs to play with them in a game of catch. A strong caveat is that you use only those balls made especially for dogs.

It pays to invest in entertainment toys and exercise devices which are marketed particularly for dogs. These products outlast everyday play things and are much safer for your pet. The Gumaball® is a great example of a dog toy worth the price of admission.

Housebreaking is required training for all puppies and even some older dogs who come in to new homes. There are many experience-based rules for the housebreaking owner to follow, including the use of a restricted area and close supervision. If approached thoughtfully and intelligently, housebreaking should proceed smoothly to its completion.

Housebreaking and Training

HOUSEBREAKING

The new addition to your family may already have received some basic house training before his arrival in your home. If he has not, remember that a puppy will want to relieve himself about half a dozen times a day; it is up to you to specify where and when he should "do his business." Housebreaking is your first training concern and should begin the moment you bring the puppy home.

Ideally, puppies should be taken outdoors after meals, as a full stomach will exert pressure on the bladder and colon. What

The value of the news may be waning in recent years, but newspaper will always have a worthwhile purpose to the new dog owner.

goes into the dog must eventually come out; the period after his meal is the most natural and appropriate time. When he eliminates, he should be praised, for this will increase the likelihood of the same thing happening after every meal. He should also be encouraged to that your pet will associate the act of elimination with a particular word of your choice rather than with a particular time or place which might not always be convenient or available. So whether you are visiting an unfamiliar place or don't want to go outside with your dog in sub-

Housebreaking pads, used by many cautious owners instead of the ever trusty press, can be purchased in pet shops and pet supply outlets.

use the same area and will probably be attracted to it after frequent use.

Some veterinarians maintain that a puppy can learn to urinate and defecate on command, if properly trained. The advantage of this conditioning technique is zero temperatures, he will still be able to relieve himself when he hears the specific command word. Elimination will occur after this "trigger" phrase or word sets up a conditioned reflex in the dog, who will eliminate anything contained in his bladder or bowel upon hearing it. The shorter the word, the more you can repeat it and imprint it on your dog's memory.

Your chosen command word should be given simultaneously with the sphincter opening events in order to achieve perfect and rapid conditioning. This is why it is important to familiarize yourself with the tell-tale signs preceding your puppy's elimination process. Then you will be prepared to say the word at the crucial moment. There is usually a sense of urgency on the dog's part; he will soon learn to associate the act with the word. One word of advice, however, if you plan to try out this method: never use the puppy's name or any other word which he might frequently hear about the house—you can imagine the result!

Finally, remember that any training takes time. Such a conditioned response can be obtained with intensive practice with any normal, healthy dog over six weeks of age. Even Pavlov's salivating dogs required fifty repetitions before the desired response was achieved.

Crates assist in potty-training the puppy. The dog's natural instinct is never to soil his sleeping area.

may follow a sniffing and circling pattern which you will soon recognize. It is important to use the command in his usual area only when you know the puppy can eliminate, i.e., when his stomach or bladder is full. He

Patience and persistence will eventually produce results—do not lose heart!

Indoors, sheets of newspapers can be used to cover the specific area where your dog should relieve himself. These should be placed some distance away from his sleeping and feeding area, as a puppy will not urinate or defecate where he eats. When the newspapers are changed, the bottom papers should be placed on top of the new ones in order to reinforce the purpose of

the run of the house, the sheer size of the place will seem overwhelming and confusing and he might leave his "signature" on your furniture or clothes! There will be time later to familiarize him gradually with his new surroundings.

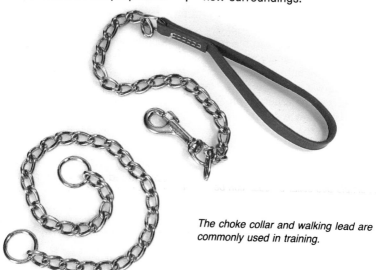

The choke collar and walking lead are commonly used in training.

the papers by scent as well as by sight. The puppy should be praised during or immediately after he has made use of this particular part of the room. Each positive reinforcement increases the possibility of his using that area again.

When he arrives, it is advisable to limit the puppy to one room, usually the kitchen, as it most likely has a linoleum or easily washable floor surface. Given

PATIENCE, PERSISTENCE, AND PRAISE

As with a human baby, you must be patient, tolerant, and understanding of your pet's mistakes, making him feel loved and wanted, not rejected and isolated. You wouldn't hit a baby for soiling his diapers, as you would realize that he was not yet able to control his bowel movements; be as compassionate with your canine infant. Never rub his nose in his excreta. Never indulge in the common practice of punishing him with a rolled-up newspaper. Never hit a puppy with your hand. He will only become "hand-shy" and learn to fear you. Usually the punishment is meted out sometime after the offense and loses its efficacy, as the bewildered dog cannot connect the two events. Moreover, by association, he will soon learn to be afraid of you and anything to do with newspapers—including, perhaps, that area where he is *supposed* to relieve himself!

A simple dog collar or leash can be deceiving. Never be afraid to ask your pet shop proprietor exactly how a particular device is intended to work.

Most puppies are eager to please. Praise, encouragement, and reward (particularly the food variety) will produce far better results than any scolding or physical punishment. Moreover, it is far better to dissuade your puppy from doing certain things, such as chewing on chair legs or other furniture, by making those objects particularly distasteful to him. Some pet shops stock bitter apple sprays or citronella compounds for application to furniture legs. These products are generally safer than old-fashioned home remedies. An owner may soon discover that application of these products may indeed make it seem as if the object itself was administering the punishment whenever he attempted to chew it. He probably wouldn't need a second reminder and your furniture will remain undamaged.

Remember that the reason a dog has housebreaking or behavior problems is because his owner has allowed them to develop. This is why you must begin as you intend to continue, letting your dog know what is acceptable and unacceptable behavior. It is also important that you be consistent in your

A choke collar can be an effective training tool when properly used.

demands; you cannot feed him from the dining room table one day and then punish him when he begs for food from your dinner guests.

TRAINING

You will want the newest member of your family to be welcomed by everyone; this will not happen if he urinates in every room of the house or barks all night! He needs training in the correct forms of behavior in this new human world. You cannot expect your puppy to become the perfect pet overnight. He needs your help in his socialization process. Training greatly facilitates and enhances the relationship of the dog to his owner and to the rest of society. A successfully trained dog can be taken anywhere and behave well with anyone. Indeed, it is that one crucial word—*training*—which can transform an aggressive animal into a peaceful, well-behaved pet. Now, how does this "transformation" take place?

WHEN AND HOW TO TRAIN

Like housebreaking, training should begin as soon as the puppy enters the house. The formal training sessions should be short but frequent, for example, ten to fifteen minute periods three times a day. These are much more effective than long, tiring sessions of half an hour which might soon become boring. You are building your relationship with your puppy during these times, so make them as enjoyable as possible. It is a good idea to have these sessions *before* the puppy's meal, not after it when he wouldn't feel like exerting himself; the dog will then associate something pleasurable with his training sessions and look forward to them.

THE COLLAR AND LEASH

Your puppy should become used to a collar and leash as soon as possible. If he is very young, a thin, choke-chain collar can be used, but you will need a larger and heavier one for training when he is a little older. Remember to have his name and address on an identification tag attached to his collar, as you don't want to lose your pet if he should happen to leave your premises and explore the neighborhood!

Nylon and leather leads are the most popular with pet owners.

Let the puppy wear his collar until he is used to how it feels. After a short time he will soon become accustomed to it and you can attach the leash. He might resist your attempts to lead him or simply sit down and refuse to budge. Fight him for a few minutes, tugging on the leash if necessary, then let him relax for the day. He won't be trained until he learns that he must obey the pull under any circumstance, but this will take a few sessions. Remember that a dog's period of concentration is short, so LITTLE and OFTEN is the wisest course of action—and patience is the password to success.

For safety purposes, as well as the comfort of your pet, be sure to choose the right-sized collar and a sensible leash for your daily walks.

GIVING COMMANDS

When you begin giving your puppy simple commands, make them as short as possible and use the same word with the same meaning at all times, for example, "Heel," "Sit," and "Stay." You must be consistent; otherwise your puppy will become confused. The dog's name should prefix all commands to attract his attention. Do not become impatient with him however many times you have to repeat your command.

A good way to introduce the "Come" command is by calling the puppy when his meal is ready. Once this is learned, you can call your pet to you at will, always remembering to praise him for his prompt obedience. This "reward," or positive reinforcement, is such a crucial part of training that a Director of the New York Academy of Dog Training constructed his whole teaching program upon the methods of "Love, Praise, and Reward." Incidentally, if you use the command "Come," use it every time. Don't switch to "Come here" or "Come boy," as this will only confuse your dog.

It is worth underlining the fact that punishment is an ineffective teaching technique. We have already seen this in housebreaking. For example, if your pup should run away, it would be senseless to beat him when he eventually returns; he would only connect the punishment with his return, not with running away! In addition, it is unwise to call him to you to punish him, as he will soon learn not to respond when you call his name.

Harnesses can be used for daily walks, though some dogs do not find them comfortable. Heavily coated dogs especially may object, and the harness can eventually wear on the dog's coat.

Housebreaking and Training

SOME SPECIFIC COMMANDS

"Sit" This is one of the easiest and most useful commands for your dog to learn, so it is a good idea to begin with it. The only equipment required is a leash, a collar, and a few tasty tidbits. Take your dog out for some exercise before his meal. After about five minutes, call him to you, praise him when he arrives,

Praise must be given when the dog correctly assumes the sit position. If praise is given before sitting or after the dog makes motion to rise, the dog may become confused.

and slip his collar on him. Hold the leash tightly in your right hand; this should force the dog's head up and focus his attention on you. As you say "Sit" in a loud, clear voice, with your left hand press steadily on his rump until he is in a sitting position. As soon as he is in the correct position, praise him and give him the tidbit you have in your hand. Now wait a few minutes to let him rest and repeat the routine. Through repetition, the dog soon associates the word with the act. Never make the lesson too long. Eventually your praise will be reward enough for your puppy. Other methods to teach this command exist, but this one, executed with care and moderation, has proven the most effective.

"Sit-Stay/Stay" To teach your pet to remain in one place or "stay" on your command, first of all order him to the sitting position at your side. Lower your left hand with the flat of your palm in front of his nose and your fingers pointing downwards. Hold the leash high and taut behind his head so that he cannot move. Speak the command "Sit-stay" and, as you are giving it, step in front of him. Repeat the command and tighten the leash so the animal cannot follow you. Walk completely around him, repeating the command and keeping him

notionless by holding the leash
at arm's length above him to
check his movement. When he
remains in this position for about
fifteen seconds, you can begin
the second part of the training.
You will have to exchange the
leash for a nylon cord or rope
about twenty to thirty feet long.
Repeat the whole routine from
the beginning and be ready to
prevent any movement towards
you with a sharp "Sit-stay."
Move around him in ever-
widening circles until you are
about fifteen feet away from him.
If he still remains seated, you
can pat yourself on the back!
One useful thing to remember is
that the dog makes associations
with what you say, how you say
it, and what you do while you are
saying it. Give this command in a
firm, clear tone of voice, perhaps
using an admonishing forefinger
raised, warning the dog to
"stay."

"Heel" When you walk your dog,
you should hold the leash firmly
in your right hand. The dog
should walk on your left so you
have the leash crossing your
body. This enables you to have
greater control over the dog.

Let your dog lead you for the
first few moments so that he fully
understands that freedom can
be his if he goes about it
properly. He already knows that
when he wants to go outdoors
the leash and collar are

*Timing is all-important in sit training—
be sure to say "sit" and press down on
the dog's rump at the same time.*

necessary, so he has respect for
the leash. Now, if he starts to
pull in one direction while
walking, all you do is *stop
walking.* He will walk a few steps
and then find that he can't walk
any further. He will then turn and
look into your face. *This is the
crucial point!* Just stand there for
a moment and stare right back at
him . . . now walk another ten
feet and stop again. Again your
dog will probably walk to the end
of the leash, find he can't go any
further, and turn around and look
again. If he starts to pull and

jerk, just stand there. After he quiets down, bend down and comfort him, as he may be frightened. Keep up this training until he learns not to outwalk you.

Once the puppy obeys the pull of the leash, half of your training is accomplished. "Heeling" is a necessity for a well-behaved dog, so teach him to walk beside you, head even with your knee. Nothing looks sadder than a big dog taking his helpless owner for a walk. It is annoying to passers-by and other dog owners to have a large dog, however friendly, bear down on them and entangle dogs, people, and packages.

To teach your dog, start off walking briskly, saying "Heel" in a firm voice. Pull back with a sharp jerk if he lunges ahead, and if he lags repeat the command and tug on the leash, not allowing him to drag behind. After the dog has learned to heel at various speeds on leash, you can remove it and practice heeling free, but have it ready to snap on again as soon as he wanders.

"Come" Your dog has already learned to come to you when you call his name. Why? Because you only call him when his food is ready or when you wish to play with him or praise him. Outdoors such a response is more difficult to achieve, if he is happily

When in the heel position, the dog should be at your left side. The lead should be held in your right hand, loosely except when checking him back to the desired position.

playing by himself or with other dogs, so he must be trained to come to you when he is called. To teach him to come, let him reach the end of a long lead, then give the command, gently pulling him towards you at the same time. As soon as he associates the word *come* with the action of moving towards you, pull only when he does not respond immediately. As he starts to come, move back to make him learn that he must come from a distance as well as when he is close to you. Soon you may be able to practice without a leash, but if he is slow to come or actively disobedient, go to him and pull him toward you, repeating the command. Always remember to reward his successful completion of a task.

"Down" Teaching the "down" command ideally begins while your dog is still a pup. During

Be gentle and reassuring with your dog, especially during the early stages of the down training—he may not understand what you are doing and may even feel threatened.

Correct behavior deserves positive reinforcement. When your dog heels, let him know how pleased you are by giving a kind word or reward.

puppyhood your dog frequently will lie down, as this position is one of the dog's most natural positions. Invest some time, and keep close watch over your pup. Each time he begins to lie, repeat in a low convincing tone the word "down." If for the first day of training, you concur a majority of the dog's sitting with your commands and continue with reinforcement and moderate praise your pup should conquer the "down" command in no time.

Teaching the "down" command to a mature dog likely will require more effort. Although the lying position is still natural to a dog, his being forced into it is not. Some dogs may react with

Once he is in the correct down position, lavish praise will tell him that he is doing well.

fear, anger, or confusion. Others may accept the process and prove quick learners. Have your dog sit and face you. If he is responsive and congenial, gently take his paws, and slowly pull them towards you; give the "down" command as he approaches the proper position. Repeat several times: moderate reinforcement of this procedure should prove successful.

For the dog that responds with anger or aggression, attach a lead (and a muzzle) and have the dog sit facing you at a close distance. There should be a J-loop formed by the lead. With moderate force, relative to the size and strength of your dog, step on the J-loop, forcing the dog down, while repeating the command "down" in a low forceful tone. When the dog is down, moderate praise should be given. If the dog proves responsive, you may attempt extending his legs to the "down" position—leaving the muzzle on, of course. Daily reinforcement of the training method will soon yield the desired results. The keys to remember are: patience, persistence, and praise.

Behavior Modification

"Problems with the Barking Dog" and "Aggressive Behavior and Dominance" are extracts from the veterinary monograph *Canine Behavior* (a compilation of columns from *Canine Practice,* a journal published by Veterinary Practice Publishing Company).

PROBLEMS WITH THE BARKING DOG

One of the most frequent complaints about canine behavior is barking. Aside from the biting dog, the barking dog is probably the pet peeve of many non-dog owners. I know of at least one city in which owners of dogs that bark excessively, and for which there are complaints on file, are required to take steps to eliminate the barking.

Canine practitioners are drawn into problems with barking when they are asked for their advice in helping an owner come up with a solution or, as a last resort, when they are requested to perform a debarking operation or even euthanasia. In this column I will deal with some of the factors that apparently cause dogs to bark and suggest some corrective approaches.

Barking is, of course, a natural response for many dogs. They have an inherited predisposition to bark as an alarm when other dogs or people approach their territory. Alarm barking makes

Only in the most extreme situations may trainers recommend electric-shock collars for correcting a dog's misbehavior.

many dogs valuable as household watchdogs and is not necessarily undesirable behavior. With a different vocal tone and pattern, dogs bark when they are playing with each other. On occasion dogs have a tendency to bark back at other dogs or join in with other barking dogs.

In addition to inherited barking tendencies, dogs can also learn to bark if the barking is followed, at least sometimes, by a reward. Thus dogs may bark when they wish to come in the house or to get out of a kennel. Some dogs are trained to bark upon hearing the command "speak" for a food reward.

One of the first approaches to take when discussing a barking problem is to determine if the behavior is a manifestation of a natural (inherited) tendency or is learned behavior which has been rewarded in the past.

praise again when it barks after being told to "speak," it will eventually stop this type of barking. This is the process of extinction and it implies that the behavior must be repeated but never again rewarded.

A more practical example of the possible use of extinction

Canine viciousness cannot be tolerated. Owners who train their dogs to be vicious are to blame for the strong anti-dog sentiment in our communities.

Can Barking Be Extinguished?

Extinction, as a way of eliminating a behavioral problem, may be considered when it is clear that the behavior has been learned and when one can identify the specific rewarding or reinforcing factors that maintain the behavior.

For example, the dog that barks upon hearing the command "speak" is periodically rewarded with food and praise. If a dog is never, ever given food or

would be in dealing with the dog that apparently barks because, at least occasionally, it is allowed in the house. By not allowing the dog in the house until the barking has become very frequent and loud, the owners may have shaped the barking behavior to that which is the most objectionable. If the dog is never allowed in the house again when barking, the barking should eventually be extinguished—at least theoretically.

How Should Punishment Be Used?

Sometimes it is not feasible to attempt to extinguish barking even if it seems to be the case that the behavior was learned. This brings up the advisability of punishment. Clients who seek advice in dealing with a barking problem may already have employed some type of punishment such as shouting at the dog or throwing something at it. That this type of punishment is ineffective is attested to by the fact that the client is seeking advice. By shouting at a dog or hitting, a person interferes with what effect the punishment may have on the behavior itself through the arousal of autonomic reactions and escape attempts or submissive responses by the dog.

The Water Bucket Approach

I am rather impressed by the ingenuity of some dog owners in

Sound-wave bark-control collars emit a noise that is inaudible to man but discomforting to the canine. These should not be used without professional supervision.

coming up with ways to punish a dog for barking without being directly involved in administering the punishment. One such harried dog owner I talked to, who was also a veterinarian, was plagued by his dog's barking in the kennel commencing at about 1:30 a.m. every night. A platform to hold a bucket of water was constructed over the area of the kennel in which the dog usually chose to bark. Through a system of hinges, ropes, and pulleys, a mechanism was devised so that the dog owner could pull a rope from his bedroom window, dumping a bucket of water on the dog when he started to bark. The bucket was suspended such that once it was dumped, it

Muzzles may prevent biting, but the root cause of biting must be extracted if the dog is to live as a trusted member of the human family.

uprighted itself and the owner could fill it again remotely by turning on a garden hose. After two appropriate dunkings, the dog's barking behavior was apparently eliminated.

In advising a client on the type of punishment discussed above, keep in mind one important consideration. From the time the owner is ready to administer punishment for barking, every attempt should be made to punish all undesirable barking from that point on and not to allow excessively long periods of barking to go unpunished. Thus it may be necessary to keep a dog indoors when away unless the dog will be punished for barking when the owner is gone.

Alternative Responses Barking dogs are, and probably always will be, one of the enduring problems of dog owners. Barking is relatively effortless, and it is such a natural response for many dogs that it is admittedly hard to eliminate with either punishment or a program of conditioning non-barking. In some instances it may be advisable to forget about eliminating barking and to suggest that the problem be dealt with by changing the circumstances which lead to barking. For example, a dog that

Pet gates are used to confine a dog to certain areas of the house. The dog must learn to accept any such restrictions and not attempt to overcome them.

barks continuously in the backyard while the owners are away may not bark if left in the house while they are gone. But the problem of keeping the dog in the house may be related to inadequate house training or the dog's shedding hair or climbing onto the furniture. It may be easier to correct these latter behavioral problems than it is to change the barking behavior.

AGGRESSIVE BEHAVIOR AND DOMINANCE

Aggressiveness can have many causes. Determining what kind of aggression an animal is manifesting is a prerequisite to successful treatment of the behavior. A frequent problem that is presented to the practitioner is one of aggression related to dominance.

Dogs, which are social animals, have a hierarchal system of dominance within their pack. This predisposition to take a dominant or submissive position relative to fellow canines also occurs in relationship to people. Only in unusual situations would a submissive dog threaten a dominant animal, and almost never would it physically assault its superior. The dominant dog, however, frequently threatens submissive individuals to maintain its position. In a household setting, a person may be the object of threats, and when the person backs off, the dog's position is reassured. The aggressive behavior is also reinforced, and when behavior is reinforced it is likely to recur.

Case History The following is a typical case history of a dog presented for aggression stemming from dominance.

Max was a two-year-old intact male Cocker Spaniel. He had been acquired by Mr. Smith, one year prior to his owner's marriage, as a puppy. He liked and was well liked by both Mr. and Mrs. Smith. He frequently solicited and received attention from both people. However, several times over the last few months, Max had snapped at Mrs. Smith and repeatedly growled at her. A detailed anamnesis revealed that such incidents usually occurred in situations where the dog wanted his own way or did not want to be bothered. He would growl if asked to move off a chair or if persistently commanded to do a specific task. He growled if Mrs. Smith came between him and a young female Cocker Spaniel acquired a year ago. He also refused to let Mrs. Smith take anything from his possession. Max never showed any of these aggressive behaviors toward Mr. Smith or strangers. Admittedly he did not have much opportunity to demonstrate such

behaviors toward strangers. A description of the dog's body and facial postures and circumstances under which the aggression occurred did not indicate that this was a case of fear-induced aggression, but rather one of assertion of dominance.

Mrs. Smith's reaction to the aggression was always to retreat, and, hence, the dog was rewarded for his assertiveness. She had never physically disciplined the dog and was afraid to do so. To encourage her to physically take control of the dog would likely have resulted in her being bitten. The dominance-submissive relationship had to be reversed in a more subtle manner.

Instructions to Client Mrs. Smith was instructed to avoid all situations which might evoke any aggressive signs from Max. This was to prevent any further reinforcement of his growling and threats.

Both she and her husband were not to indiscriminately pet or show affection towards the dog. For the time being, if Max solicited attention from Mr. Smith, he was to ignore the dog. Mrs. Smith was to take advantage of Max's desire for attention by giving him a command which he had to obey before she praised and petted him. She was also to take advantage of high motivation levels for other activities whenever such situations arose. Max had to obey a command before she gave him anything—before she petted him, before she let him out or in, etc.

Mrs. Smith also was to assume total care of the dog and coveted food rewards as well as praise. These were entirely fun and play sessions—but within a few days the dog had acquired the habit of quickly responding to commands. And this habit transferred over to the non-game situations.

There is a wide variety of collars and harnesses available to the dog owner. Talk with your pet shop proprietor to determine which one best satisfies your needs.

become "the source of all good things in life" for Max. She was to feed him, take him on walks, play with him, etc.

Mrs. Smith also spent 5–10 minutes a day teaching Max simple parlor tricks and obedience responses for

Results Within a few weeks, Max had ceased to growl and threaten Mrs. Smith in situations that he previously had. He would move out of her way or lie quietly when she would pass by him. She could order him off the furniture and handle the female

Behavior Modification

Cocker Spaniel without eliciting threats from Max.

Mrs. Smith still felt that she would not be able to take the objects from Max's possession. Additional instructions were given to her. She then began placing a series of objects at progressively closer distances to the dog while the dog was in a sit-stay position. After she placed the object on the floor for a short time, she would pick it up. If the dog was still in a sit-stay (which it always was), he received a reward of cheese and verbal praise. Eventually the objects were to be placed and removed from directly in front of the dog. At first she was to use objects that the dog did not care much about and then progressively use more coveted items. This was what she was

Treats can be effective in shaping behavior and establishing a rapport with your pet.

supposed to do, but before she actually had completed the program she called in excitedly to report that she had taken a piece of stolen food and a household ornament from Max's mouth. And he didn't even object! She said she had calmly told Max to sit. He did. He was so used to doing so, in the game and other situations, that the response was now automatic. She walked over, removed the item from his mouth, and praised him.

Mrs. Smith did resume the systematic presentation of objects and put the dog on an intermittent schedule of food and praise reinforcement during the practice sessions. Mr. Smith again began interacting with Max.

A progress check six months later indicated Max was still an obedient dog and had definitely assumed a submissive position relative to both of his owners. The dominance hierarchy between Max and Mrs. Smith had been reversed *without resorting to any physical punishment.* Mrs. Smith was instructed to reinforce her dominance position by frequently giving Max a command and reinforcing him for the appropriate response.

Summary The essential elements in treatment of such cases are as follows. First, of course, there must be a correct

Owners must take an active part in shaping their dog's behavior. Providing a sensible chew device can help alleviate an animal's frustration and thereby eliminate some undesirable behavior.

diagnosis of what kind of aggressive behavior is occurring. During the course of treatment, the submissive person(s) should avoid all situations that might evoke an aggressive attitude by the dog. All other family members should totally ignore the dog during the treatment interim. The person most dominated by the dog should take over complete care of the dog in addition to spending 5–10 minutes a day teaching the dog tricks or simple obedience commands (sit-stay is a useful one to gain control of the dog in subsequent circumstances). These should be fun-and-games

situations. Food rewards are highly recommended in addition to simple praise.

The person submissive to the dog should take the opportunity to give the dog a command, which must be obeyed, before doing anything pleasant for the dog.

It must be emphasized to the owner that no guarantee can be made that the dog will never threaten or be aggressive again. What is being done, as with all other aggression cases, is an attempt to reduce the likelihood, incidence, and intensity of occurrence of the aggressive behavior.

DESTRUCTIVE TENDENCIES

It is ironical but true that a dog's destructive behavior in the home may be proof of his love for his owner. He may be trying to get more attention from his owner or, in other cases, may be expressing his frustration at his owner's absence. An abundance of unused energy may also contribute to a dog's destructive behavior, and therefore the owner should ensure that his dog has, at least, twenty minutes of vigorous exercise a day.

As a dog's destructive tendencies may stem from his desire to get more attention from his owner, the latter should devote specific periods each day to his dog when he is actively interacting with him. Such a period should contain practice obedience techniques during which the owner can reward the dog with his favorite food as well as praise and affection.

Planned departure conditioning is one specific technique which has been used to solve the problem of destructive tendencies in a puppy. It eventually ensures the dog's good behavior during the owner's absence. A series of short departures, which are identical to real departures, should condition the dog to behave well in the owner's absence. How is this to be achieved? Initially, the departures are so short (2–5 minutes) that the dog has no opportunity to be destructive. The dog is always rewarded for having been good when the owner returns. Gradually the duration of the departures is increased. The departure time is also varied so that the dog does not know when the owner is going to return. Since a different kind of behavior is now expected, it is best if a new stimulus or "atmosphere" is introduced into the training sessions to permit the dog to distinguish these departures as different from previous departures when he was destructive.

This new stimulus could be the sound of the radio or television. The association which the dog will develop is that whenever the "signal" or "stimulus" is on, the owner will return in an unknown period of time and, if the dog has not been destructive, he will be rewarded. As with the daily owner-dog interaction, the food reward is especially useful.

If the dog misbehaves during his owner's absence, the owner should speak sternly to him and isolate him from social contact for at least thirty minutes. (Puppies hate to be ignored.) Then the owner should conduct another departure of a shorter time and generously reward good behavior when he returns. The owner should progress slowly enough in the program so that once the departure has been initiated, the dog is never given an opportunity to make a mistake.

If planned departures are working satisfactorily, the departure time may gradually be extended to several hours. To reduce the dog's anxiety when left alone, he should be given a "safety valve" such as the indestructible Nylabone® to play with and chew on.

While crates may be used principally for sleeping and traveling, some owners might opt to employ a crate for disciplining a dog, rather like sending a naughty child to his room.

Health Care

From the moment you purchase your puppy, the most important person in both your lives becomes your veterinarian. His

Bandaging a minor cut on the paw pad is one of many basic first-aid techniques that the dog owner should learn.

professional advice and treatment will ensure the good health of your pet. The vet is the first person to call when illness or accidents occur. Do *not* try to be your own veterinarian or apply human remedies to canine diseases. However, just as you would keep a first aid kit handy for minor injuries sustained by members of your family at home, so you should keep a similar kit prepared for your pet.

First aid for your dog would consist of stopping any bleeding, cleaning the wound, and preventing infection. Thus your kit might contain medicated powder, gauze bandages, and adhesive tape to be used in case of cuts. If the cut is deep and bleeding profusely, the bandage should be applied very tightly to help in the formation of a clot. A tight bandage should not be kept in place longer than necessary, so take your pet to the veterinarian immediately.

Walking or running on a cut pad prevents the cut from

Thoroughly clean the injury with peroxide and apply an antibiotic. Then place the injured pad in sterile gauze, secure with first-aid tape, and replace daily.

healing. Proper suturing of the cut and regular changing of the bandages should have your pet's wound healed in a week to ten days. A minor cut should be covered with a light bandage, for you want as much air as possible to reach the wound. Do not apply wads of cotton to a wound, as they will stick to the area and may cause contamination.

You should also keep some hydrogen peroxide available, as it is useful in cleaning wounds and is also one of the best and simplest emetics known. Cotton applicator swabs are useful for applying ointment or removing debris from the eyes. A pair of tweezers should also be kept handy for removing foreign bodies from the dog's neck, head or body.

Nearly everything a dog might contract in the way of sickness has basically the same set of symptoms: loss of appetite, diarrhea, dull eyes, dull coat, warm and/or runny nose, and a high temperature. Therefore, it is most important to take his temperature at the first sign of illness. To do this, you will need a rectal thermometer which should be lubricated with petroleum jelly. Carefully insert it into the rectum, holding it in place for at least two minutes. It must be held firmly; otherwise there is the danger of its being sucked up into the rectum or slipping out, thus giving an

The normal temperature for the average dog ranges from 101°F to 102.5°F. This may vary during sleeping and exercise time.

inaccurate reading. The normal temperature for a dog is between 101° and 102.5°F. If your pet is seriously ill or injured in an accident, your veterinarian will advise you what to do before he arrives.

SWALLOWING FOREIGN OBJECTS

Most of us have had experience with a child swallowing a foreign object. Usually it is a small coin; occasionally it may be a fruit pit or something more dangerous. Dogs, *as a general rule,* will not swallow anything which isn't edible. There are, however, many dogs that swallow pebbles or small shiny objects such as pins, coins, and bits of cloth and plastic. This is especially true of dogs that are offered so-called "chew toys."

Chew toys are available in many sizes, shapes, colors and materials. Some even have whistles which sound when the dog's owner plays with it or when the dog chomps on it quickly. Most dogs attack the whistle first, doing everything possible to make it stop squeaking. Obviously, if the whistle is made of metal, a dog can injure its mouth, teeth, or tongue. Therefore, *never* buy a "squeak toy" made with a metal whistle.

Other chew toys are made of vinyl, a cheap plastic which is soft to the touch and pliable. Most of the cute little toys that are figures of animals or people are made of this cheap plastic. They are sometimes hand-painted in countries where the cost of such labor is low. Not only is the paint used dangerous to dogs, because of the lead content, but the vinyl tears easily and is usually destroyed by the dog during the first hour. Small bits of vinyl may be ingested and cause blockage of the intestines. You are, therefore, reminded of these things before you buy anything vinyl for your dog!

Very inexpensive dog toys, usually found in supermarkets and other low-price venues, may

Natural chew bones can splinter and become lodged in a dog's throat. Nylon and polyurethane bones are safer for canine use.

Old discardable shoes should not be included in the dog's toy box. Such items are dangerous to a puppy or an adult dog.

be made of polyethylene. These are to be avoided completely, as this cheap plastic is, for some odd reason, attractive to dogs. Dogs destroy the toy in minutes and sometimes swallow the indigestible bits and pieces that come off. Most pet shops carry only safe toys.

WHAT TOYS ARE SAFE FOR DOGS?

Hard Rubber Toys made of hard rubber are usually safe for dogs, providing the toy is made of 100% hard rubber and not a compound of rubber and other materials. The rubber must be "virgin" and not re-ground from old tires, tubes, and other scrap rubber products. The main problem with rubber, even 100% virgin rubber, is that it oxidizes quickly, especially when subjected to the ultraviolet rays of the sun and a dog's saliva. The rubber then tends to be brittle, to crack, to dust off, and to be extremely dangerous to dogs that like swallowing things.

Nylon Toys Toys made of nylon could well be the safest of all toys, *providing the nylon is annealed*. Nylon that is not annealed is very fragile, and if you smash it against a hard surface, it might shatter like glass. The same is true when the weather is cold and the nylon drops below freezing. Thus far there is only one line of dog toys that is made of annealed virgin nylon—Nylabone®. These toys not only are annealed but they are flavored and scented. The flavors and scents, such as hambone, are undetectable by humans, but dogs seem to find them attractive.

Some nylon bones have the flavor sprayed on them or molded into them. These cheaper bones are easy to detect—just smell them. If you

The Puppy Bone® by Nylabone® is multi-purpose, designed for teething, chew-pacification, teeth-cleaning and the elimination of behavioral problems before they become habitual.

discern an odor, you know they are poorly made. The main problem with the nylon toys that have an odor is that they are not annealed and they "smell up"

the house or car. The dog's saliva dilutes the odor of the bone, and when he drops it on your rug, this odor attaches itself to the rug and is quite difficult to remove.

Annealed nylon may be the best there is, but it is not 100% safe. The Nylabone® dog chews are really meant to be Pooch Pacifiers®. This trade name indicates the effect intended for the dog, which is to relieve the tension in your excited puppy or anxious adult dog. Instead of chewing up the furniture or some other object, he chews up his Nylabone® instead. Many dogs ignore the Nylabone® for weeks, suddenly attacking it when they have to relieve their doggie tensions.

The Nylabone® is designed for the most aggressive chewers. Even so, owners should be wary that some dogs may have jaws strong enough to chomp off a piece of Nylabone®, but this is extremely rare. *One word of caution:* the Nylabone® should be replaced when the dog has chewed down the knuckle. Most dogs slowly scrape off small slivers of nylon which pass harmlessly through their digestive tract. The resultant frizzled bone actually becomes a toothbrush.

One of the great characteristics of nylon bones is that they can be boiled and sterilized. If a dog loses interest in his Nylabone®, or it is too hard for him to chew due to his age and the condition of his teeth, you can cook it in some chicken or beef broth, allowing it to boil for 30 minutes. Let it cool down normally. It will then be perfectly sterile and re-flavored for the next dog. *Don't try this with plastic bones, as they will melt and ruin your pot.*

Polyurethane Toys Because polyurethane bones such as the Gumabone® are constructed of the strongest *flexible* materials known, some dogs (and their owners) actually prefer them to the traditional nylon bones. There are several brands on the market: ignore the ones which have scents that you can discern. Some of the scented polyurethane bones have an unbearable odor after the scent has rubbed off the bone and onto your rug or car seat. Again, look for the better-quality polyurethane toy. Gumabone® is a flexible material, the same as used for making artificial hearts and the bumpers on automobiles, thus it is strong and stable. It is not as strong as Nylabone®, but many dogs like it because it is soft.

If your dog is soft-mouthed and a less aggressive, more playful chewer, he will love the great taste and fun feel of the Gumabone® products.

The most popular of the

Gumabone® products made in polyurethane are the tug toys, knots, balls, and Frisbee® flying discs. These items are almost clear in color, have the decided advantage of lasting a long time, and are useful in providing exercise for both a dog and his master or mistress.

Gumabone® is available in different sizes and shapes. These are probably the most popular of all chew toys because dogs love them.

Gumabone® has also introduced new spiral-shaped dental devices under the name Plaque Attacker®. These unique products are fast becoming standards for all aggressive chewers. The Plaque Attacker Dental Device® comes in four fun sizes and each is designed to maximize gum and teeth

Attacker® products are patented and scented with hambone to make them even more enticing for the dog. Clinical findings support the assertion that a significant reduction in calculus accompanies use of the Gumbone® products.

Whatever dog toy you buy, be sure it is high quality. Pet shops

The Plaque Attacker® is a Dental Ball™, not just a plaything, designed to reduce plaque and tartar by use of its revolutionary "dental tips."

massage through its upraised "dental tips," which pimple the surface of the toy. Similarly, the Plaque Attacker Dental Ball® ensures a reduction in plaque and tartar. This one-of-a-kind product provides hours of fun for a dog. It bounces erratically and proves to be the most exciting of all polyurethane toys. All Plaque

and certain supermarkets, as a rule, always carry the better quality toys. Of course there may be exceptions, but you are best advised to ask your local pet shop operator—or even your veterinarian—what toys are suitable for *your* dog.

In conclusion, if your dog is a swallower of foreign objects,

When emergencies occur, being prepared pays off. A first-aid kit should be accessible and always well stocked with medical accessories and supplies.

don't give him anything cheap to chew on. If he swallows a coin, you can hardly blame the Treasury! Unless your dog is carefully supervised, use only the largest size Nylabone® and Gumabone®, and replace them as soon as the dog chews down the knuckles. *Do not let the dog take the Nylabone® outdoors.* First of all he can hide and bury it, digging it up when his tensions rise. Then, too, all nylon becomes more brittle when it freezes, even Nylabone®.

IF YOUR PET SWALLOWS POISON

A poisoned dog must be treated instantly; any delay could cause his death. Different poisons act in different ways and require different treatments. If you know the dog has swallowed an acid, alkali, gasoline, or kerosene, do not induce vomiting. Give milk to dilute the poison and rush him to the vet. If you can find the bottle or container of poison, check the label to see if there is a recommended antidote. If not, try to induce vomiting by giving him a mixture of hydrogen peroxide and water. Mix the regular drugstore strength of hydrogen peroxide (3%) with an equal part of water, but do not attempt to pour it down your dog's throat, as that could cause inhalation pneumonia. Instead, simply pull the dog's lips away from the side of his mouth, making a pocket for depositing the liquid. Use at least a tablespoonful of the mixture for every ten pounds of your dog's weight. He will vomit in about two minutes. When his stomach has settled, give him a teaspoonful of Epsom salts in a little water to empty the intestine quickly. The hydrogen peroxide, on ingestion, becomes oxygen and water and is harmless to your dog; it is the best antidote for phosphorus, which is often used in rat poisons. After you have administered this emergency treatment to your pet and his stomach and bowels have been emptied, rush him to your veterinarian for further care.

The contents of a full ashtray if consumed by the curious non-smoker dog may induce nicotine poisoning. Pet owners must dog-proof their home for the safety of their animals.

DANGER IN THE HOME

There are numerous household products that can prove fatal if ingested by your pet. These include rat poison, antifreeze, boric acid, hand soap, detergents, insecticides, mothballs, household cleansers, bleaches, de-icers, polishes and disinfectants, paint and varnish removers, acetone, turpentine, and even health and beauty aids

There is another danger lurking within the home among the household plants, which are almost all poisonous, even if swallowed in small quantities. There are hundreds of poisonous plants around us, among which are: ivy leaves, cyclamen, lily of the valley, rhododendrons, tulip bulbs, azalea, wisteria, poinsettia leaves, mistletoe, daffodils,

if ingested in large enough quantities. A word to the wise should be sufficient: what you would keep locked away from your two-year-old child should also be kept hidden from your pet.

Preparing for emergencies also requires that an owner understand such basic revival techniques as cardio-pulmonary resuscitation, chest compression, heart massage, heat stroke measures, and many others.

Checking for an animal's vital signs in the event of an emergency will help you to provide the veterinarian with the answers to his preliminary questions.

jimson weed—we cannot name them all. Rhubarb leaves, for example, either raw or cooked, can cause death or violent convulsions. Peach, elderberry, and cherry trees can cause cyanide poisoning if their bark is consumed.

There are also many insects that can be poisonous to dogs such as spiders, bees, wasps, and some flies. A few toads and frogs exude a fluid that can make a dog foam at the mouth—and even kill him—if he bites too hard!

There have been cases of dogs suffering nicotine poisoning by consuming the contents of full ashtrays which thoughtless smokers have left on the coffee table. Also, do not leave nails, staples, pins, or other sharp objects lying around. Likewise, don't let your puppy play with plastic bags which could suffocate him. Unplug, remove, or cover any electrical cords or wires near your dog. Chewing live wires could lead to severe mouth burns or death. Remember that an ounce of prevention is worth a pound of cure: keep all potentially dangerous objects out of your pet's reach.

VEHICLE TRAVEL SAFETY

A dog should never be left alone in a car. It takes only a few minutes for the heat to become unbearable in the summer, and to drop to freezing in the winter.

A dog traveling in a car or truck should be well behaved. An undisciplined dog can be deadly in a moving vehicle. The dog should be trained to lie on the back seat of the vehicle. Allowing your dog to stick its head out of the window is unwise. The dog may jump or it may get something in its eye. Some manufacturers sell seat belts and car seats designed for dogs.

Traveling with your dog in the back of your pick-up truck is an unacceptable notion and dangerous to all involved.

PROTECT YOURSELF FIRST

In almost all first aid situations, the dog is in pain. He may indeed be in shock and not appear to be suffering, until you move him. Then he may bite your hand or resist being helped at all. So if you want to help your dog, help yourself first by tying his mouth closed. To do this, use a piece of strong cloth four inches wide and three feet long, depending on the size of the dog.

Car safety is a serious matter. When a dog is traveling by auto, specially designed seat belts (or the dog's crate) are the safest route.

Health Care

Make a loop in the middle of the strip and slip it over his nose with the knot under his chin and over the bony part of his nose. Pull it tight and bring the ends back around his head behind the ears and tie it tightly, ending with a bow knot for quick, easy release. Now you can handle the dog safely. As a dog perspires through his tongue, do not leave the "emergency muzzle" on any longer than necessary.

ADMINISTERING MEDICINE

When you are giving liquid medicine to your dog, it is a good idea to pull the lips away from the side of the mouth, form a lip pocket, and let the liquid trickle past the tongue. Remain at his side, never in front of the dog, as he may cough and spray you with the liquid. Moreover, you must never pour liquid medicine while the victim's tongue is drawn out, as

First aid, in the ideal sense, is the temporary care of an animal or person until professional help can be found. Recognizing the urgency in any given circumstance is the primary concern. Moving an injured animal with utmost care usually requires two persons and a clean blanket.

inhalation pneumonia could be the disastrous result.

Medicine in pill form is best administered by forcing the dog's mouth open, holding his forced to swallow the medicine. As the dog will not be feeling well, stroke his neck to comfort him and to help him swallow his medicine more easily. Do keep

Before attempting to transport an injured dog, be very careful to inspect for apparent wounds, burns or breaks while disturbing the animal as little as possible. Laying the dog in a flat position will make the carrying easier to manage.

head back, and placing the capsule as far back on his tongue as you can reach. To do this: put the palm of your hand over the dog's muzzle (his foreface) with your fingers on one side of his jaw, your thumb on the other. Press his lips hard against his teeth while using your other hand to pull down his lower jaw. With your two fingers, try to put the pill as far back on the dog's tongue as you can reach. Keep his mouth and nostrils closed and he should be an eye on him for a few moments afterward, however, to make certain that he does not spit it out.

IN CASE OF AN ACCIDENT

It is often difficult for you to assess the dog's injuries after a road accident. He may appear normal, but there might be internal hemorrhaging. A vital organ could be damaged or ribs broken. Keep the dog as quiet and warm as possible; cover him with blankets or your coat to let his own body heat build up. Signs of shock are a rapid and weak pulse, glassy-eyed appearance, subnormal temperature, and slow capillary refill time. To determine the last symptom, press firmly against the dog's gums until they turn white. Release and count the number of seconds until the gums return to their normal color. If it is more than 2–3 seconds, the dog may be going into shock. Failure to return to the reddish pink color indicates that the dog may be in serious trouble and needs immediate assistance.

If artificial respiration is required, first open the dog's mouth and check for obstructions; extend his tongue and examine the pharynx. Clear his mouth of mucus and blood and hold the mouth slightly open. Mouth-to-mouth resuscitation involves holding the dog's tongue to the bottom of his mouth with one hand and sealing his nostrils with the other while you blow into his mouth. Watch for his chest to rise with each inflation. Repeat every 5–6 seconds, the equivalent of 10–12 breaths a minute.

If the veterinarian cannot come to you, try to improvise a stretcher to take the dog to him. To carry a puppy, wrap him in a blanket that has been folded into several thicknesses. If he is in shock, it is better to pick him up

by holding one hand under his chest, the other under the hindquarters. This will keep him stretched out.

It is always better to roll an injured dog than to try and lift him. If you find him lying beside the road after a car accident, apply a muzzle even if you have to use someone's necktie to make one. Send someone for a blanket and roll him gently onto it. Two people, one on each side, can make a stretcher out of the blanket and move the dog easily.

If no blanket is available and the injured dog must be moved, try to keep him as flat as possible. So many dogs' backs are broken in car accidents that one must first consider that possibility. However, if he can move his hind legs or tail, his spine is probably not broken. Get medical assistance for him immediately.

It should be mentioned that unfortunate car accidents, which can maim or kill your dog, can be avoided if he is confined at all times either indoors or, if out-of-doors, in a fenced-in yard or some other protective enclosure. *Never* allow your dog to roam free; even a well-trained dog may, for some unknown reason, dart into the street—and the result could be tragic.

If you need to walk your dog, leash him first so that he will be protected from moving vehicles.

It is the smooth, efficient execution of first-aid technique that saves lives. Costly mistakes happen when haste and frenzy take over. When moving an injured dog, keep calm and be focused on the situation at hand. Act swiftly and maintain control at all times.

PROTECTING YOUR PET

It is important to watch for any tell-tale signs of illness so that you can spare your pet any unnecessary suffering. Your dog's eyes, for example, should normally be bright and alert, so if the haw is bloodshot or partially covers the eye, it may be a sign of illness or irritation. If your dog has matter in the corners of his eyes, bathe them with a mild eye wash; obtain ointment or eye drops from your veterinarian to treat a chronic condition.

If your dog seems to have something wrong with his ears which causes him to scratch at them or shake his head, cautiously probe the ear with a cotton swab. An accumulation of wax will probably work itself out. Dirt or dried blood, however, is indicative of ear mites or infection and should be treated immediately. Sore ears in the summer, due to insect bites, should be washed with mild soap and water, then covered with a soothing ointment and wrapped in gauze if necessary. Keep your pet away from insects until his ears heal, even if this means confining him indoors.

VACCINATION SCHEDULE

Age	Vaccination
6-8 weeks	Initial canine distemper, canine hepatitis, tracheobronchitis, canine parvovirus, as well as initial leptospirosis vaccination.
10-12 weeks	Second vaccination for all given at 6-8 weeks. Initial rabies and initial Lyme disease to be given at this time.
14-16 weeks	Third vaccination for all given at 6-8 and 10-12 weeks.Re-vaccinate annually, hereafter. Second rabies and second Lyme disease to be given at this time, and then re-vaccinated annually.

INOCULATIONS

Periodic check-ups by your veterinarian throughout your puppy's life are good health insurance. The person from whom your puppy was purchased should tell you what inoculations your puppy has had and when the next visit to the vet is necessary. You must make certain that your puppy has been vaccinated against the following infectious canine diseases: distemper, canine hepatitis, leptospirosis, rabies, parvovirus, and parainfluenza. Annual "boosters" thereafter provide inexpensive protection for your dog against such serious diseases. Puppies should also be checked for worms at an early age.

Vaccination schedules should be confirmed with your vet.

DISTEMPER

Young dogs are most susceptible to distemper, although it may affect dogs of all ages. Some signs of the disease are loss of appetite, depression, chills, and fever, as well as a watery discharge from the eyes and nose. Unless treated promptly, the disease goes into advanced stages with infections of the lungs, intestines, and nervous system. Dogs that recover may be impaired with paralysis, convulsions, a twitch, or some other defect, usually spastic in nature. Early inoculations in puppyhood should be followed by an annual booster to help protect against this disease.

CANINE HEPATITIS

The signs of hepatitis are drowsiness, loss of appetite, high temperature, and great thirst. These signs may be accompanied by swellings of the head, neck, and abdomen. Vomiting may also occur. This disease strikes quickly, and death may occur in only a few hours. An annual booster shot is needed after the initial series of puppy shots.

LEPTOSPIROSIS

Infection caused by either of two serovars, *canicola* or *copehageni,* is usually begun by the dog's licking substances contaminated by the urine or feces of infected animals. Brown rats are the main carriers of *copehageni.* The signs are weakness, vomiting, and a yellowish discoloration of the jaws, teeth, and tongue, caused by an inflammation of the kidneys. A veterinarian can administer the bacterins to protect your dog from this disease. The frequency of the doses is determined by the risk factor involved.

RABIES

This disease of the dog's central nervous system spreads by infectious saliva, which is

Lice are not a common problem in dogs and usually only infest dogs that are poorly cared for. Proper care of your dog will prevent lice infestation.

transmitted by the bite of an infected animal. Of the two main classes of signs, the first is "furious rabies," in which the dog shows a period of melancholy or depression, then irritation, and finally paralysis. The first period can be from a few hours to several days, and during this time the dog is cross and will change his position often, lose his appetite, begin to lick, and bite or swallow foreign objects. During this phase the dog is spasmodically wild and has impulses to run away. The dog acts fearless and bites everything in sight. If he is caged or confined, he will fight at the bars and possibly break teeth or fracture his jaw. His bark

The deer fly has a wicked bite that can cause a welt; all flies can carry disease and germs.

becomes a peculiar howl. In the final stage, the animal's lower jaw becomes paralyzed and hangs down. He then walks with a stagger, and saliva drips from his mouth. About four to eight days after the onset of paralysis, the dog dies.

The second class of symptoms is referred to as "dumb rabies" and is characterized by the dog's walking in a bearlike manner with his head down. The lower jaw is paralyzed and the dog is unable to bite. It appears as if he has a bone caught in his throat.

If a dog is bitten by a rabid animal, he probably can be saved if he is taken to a veterinarian in time for a series of injections. After the signs appear, however, no cure is possible. The local health department must be notified in the case of a rabid dog, for he is a danger to all who come near him. As with the other shots each year, an annual rabies inoculation is very important. In many areas, the administration of rabies vaccines for dogs is required by law.

PARVOVIRUS

This relatively new virus is a contagious disease that has spread in almost epidemic proportions throughout certain sections of the United States. It has also appeared in Australia, Canada, and Europe. Canine parvovirus attacks the intestinal tract, white blood cells, and heart muscle. It is believed to spread through dog-to-dog contact, and the specific course of infection seems to come from fecal matter of infected dogs. Overcoming parvovirus is difficult, for it is capable of existing in the environment for many months under varying conditions and temperatures, and it can be transmitted from place to place on the hair and feet of infected dogs, as well as on the clothes and shoes of people.

Vomiting and severe diarrhea, which will appear within five to seven days after the animal has been exposed to the virus, are the initial signs of this disease. At the onset of illness, feces will be light gray or yellow-gray in color, and the urine might be blood-streaked. Because of the vomiting and severe diarrhea, the dog that has contracted the disease will dehydrate quickly. Depression and loss of appetite, as well as a rise in temperature, can accompany the other symptoms. Death caused by this disease usually occurs within 48 to 72 hours following the appearance of the symptoms. Puppies are hardest hit, and the virus is fatal to 75 percent of puppies that contract it. Death in puppies can be within two days of the onset of the illness.

A series of shots administered by a veterinarian is the best

The stable fly is capable of a painful bite.

preventive measure for canine parvovirus. It is also important to disinfect the area where the dog is housed by using one part sodium hypochlorite solution (household bleach) to thirty parts of water and to keep the dog from coming into contact with the fecal matter of other dogs.

LYME DISEASE
Known as a bacterial infection, Lyme disease is transmitted by ticks infected with a spirochete known as *Borrelia burgdorferi*. The disease is most often

The deer tick is a principal carrier of Lyme disease.

The brown dog tick is the most common tick found on dogs. It is much larger than a deer tick.

acquired by the parasitic bite of an infected deer tick, *Ixodes dammini*. While the range of symptoms is broad, common warning signs include: rash beginning at the bite and soon extending in a bullseye-targetlike fashion; chills, fever, lack of balance, lethargy, and stiffness; swelling and pain, especially in the joints, possibly leading to arthritis or arthritic conditions; heart problems, weak limbs, facial paralysis, and lack of tactile sensation.

Concerned dog owners, especially those living in the United States, should contact a veterinarian to discuss Lyme disease. A vaccination has been developed and is routinely administered to puppies twice before the 16th week, and then annually.

PARAINFLUENZA

Parainfluenza, or infectious canine tracheobronchitis, is commonly known as "kennel cough." It is highly contagious, affects the upper respiratory system, and is spread through direct or indirect contact with already diseased dogs. It will readily infect dogs of all ages that have not been vaccinated or that were previously infected. While this condition is definitely one of the serious diseases in dogs, it is self-limiting, usually lasting only two to four weeks.

The symptoms are high fever and intense, harsh coughing that brings up mucus. As long as your pet sees your veterinarian immediately, the chances for his complete recovery are excellent.

EXTERNAL PARASITES

A parasite is an animal that lives in or on an organism of another species, known as the host, without contributing to the well-being of the host. The majority of dogs' skin problems are parasitic in nature and an estimated 90% of puppies are born with parasites.

Ticks can cause serious problems to dogs where the latter have access to woods, fields, and vegetation in which large numbers of native mammals live. Ticks are usually found clinging to vegetation and attach themselves to animals passing by. They have eight legs and a heavy shield or shell-like covering on their upper surface. Only by keeping dogs away from tick-infested areas can ticks on dogs be prevented.

The flea is the single most common cause of skin and coat problems in dogs. There are 11,000 kinds of fleas which can transmit specific disorders like tapeworm and heartworm or transport smaller parasites onto your dog. The common tapeworm, for example, requires the flea as an intermediate host for completion of its life cycle.

Fumigating flea bombs are commonly used to de-flea a home. It is essential to follow the manufacturer's instructions to the letter, as this product's fumes can kill more than just insects.

A female flea can lay hundreds of eggs and these will become adults in less than three weeks. Depending on the temperature and the amount of moisture, large numbers of fleas can attack dogs. The ears of dogs, in particular, can play host to hundreds of fleas.

Fleas can lurk in crevices and cracks, carpets, and bedding for months, so frequent cleaning of your dog's environment is absolutely essential. If he is infected by other dogs, then have him bathed and "dipped," which means that he will be put into water containing a chemical that kills fleas. Your veterinarian will advise which dip to use, and your dog must be bathed for at least twenty minutes. These parasites are tenacious and remarkably agile creatures; fleas have existed since prehistoric times and have been found in arctic as well as tropical

Fleas are among the most common external parasites and can be real pests to eliminate from your pet.

climates. Some experts claim that fleas can jump 150 times the length of their bodies; this makes them difficult to catch and kill. Thus, treating your pet for parasites without simultaneously treating the environment is both inefficient and ineffective.

INTERNAL PARASITES

Four common internal parasites that may infect a dog are: roundworms, hookworms, whipworms, and tapeworms. The first three can be diagnosed by laboratory examination of the dog's stool, and tapeworms can be seen in the stool or attached to the hair around the anus. When a veterinarian determines what type of worm or worms are present, he then can advise the best treatment.

Roundworms, the dog's most common intestinal parasite, have a life cycle which permits complete eradication by worming twice, ten days apart. The first worming will remove all adults and the second will destroy all subsequently hatched eggs before they, in turn, can produce more parasites.

A dog in good physical condition is less susceptible to worm infestation than a weak dog. Proper sanitation and a nutritious diet help in preventing worms. One of the best preventive measures is to have clean, dry bedding for the dog, as this diminishes the possibility of reinfection due to flea or tick bites.

Heartworm infestation in dogs is passed by mosquitoes. Dogs with this disease tire easily, have difficulty in breathing, and lose weight despite a hearty appetite. Administration of preventive medicine throughout the spring, summer, and fall months is advised. A veterinarian must first take a blood sample from the dog to test for the presence of the disease, and if the dog is heartworm-free, pills or liquid medicine can be prescribed to protect against any infestation.

CANINE SENIOR CITIZENS

The processes of aging and gradual degenerative changes start far earlier in a dog than often observed, usually at about seven years of age. If we recall that each year of a dog's life roughly corresponds to about seven years in the life of a man,

The fraternity of internal parasites and their eggs: whipworms, hookworms, roundworms and tapeworms.

Health Care

by the age of seven he is well into middle age. Your pet will become less active, will have a poorer appetite with increased thirst, there will be frequent periods of constipation and less than normal passage of urine. His skin and coat might become dull and dry and his hair will become thin and fall out. There is a tendency towards obesity in old age, which should be avoided by maintaining a regular exercise program. Remember, also, that your pet will be less able to cope with extreme heat, cold, fatigue, and change in routine.

There is the possibility of loss or impairment of hearing or eyesight. He may become bad-tempered more often than in the past. Other ailments such as rheumatism, arthritis, kidney infections, heart disease, male prostatism, and hip dysplasia may occur. Of course, all these require a veterinarian's examination and recommendation of suitable treatment. Care of the teeth is

Heartworm life cycle: a carrier mosquito bites a dog and deposits microfilariae, which travel through the dog's bloodstream, lodging in the heart to reproduce. The carrier dog is later bitten by an uninfected mosquito, which becomes infected, and bites and infects another dog . . . .

Taking a dog's pulse is useful as it reflects his heartbeat. To do so is quite simple: feel along the inside of your dog's thigh at the juncture where it meets the body. Press with a finger to feel the pulsation. (Do not use your thumb.)

also important in the aging dog. Indeed, the mouth can be a barometer of nutritional health. Degenerating gums, heavy tartar on the teeth, loose teeth, and sore lips are common. The worst of all diseases in old age, however, is neglect. Good care in early life will have its effect on your dog's later years; the nutrition and general health care of his first few years can determine his lifespan and the quality of his life. It is worth bearing in mind that the older, compared to the younger, animal needs more protein of good biological value, more vitamins A, B-complex, D and E, more calcium and iron, and less fat.

An adult male mosquito. Only female mosquitoes will suck blood from a host animal.

Preventive Dental Care

ALL DOGS NEED TO CHEW

Puppies and young dogs need something with resistance to chew on while their teeth and jaws are developing—to cut the puppy teeth, to induce growth of the permanent teeth under the puppy teeth, to assist in getting

An artist's representation of the calculus index, ranging from index rating **4** (topmost drawing) *through index rating* **0** (lowest drawing).

4 *Buccal crown covered*

3 *⅔ crown covered*

2 *⅓ crown covered*

1 *Only gingival margin covered*

0 *No calculus evident*

4

3

2

1

0

rid of the puppy teeth on time, to help the permanent teeth through the gums, to assure normal jaw development and to settle the permanent teeth solidly in the jaws.

The adult dog's desire to chew stems from the instinct for tooth cleaning, gum massage, and jaw exercise—plus the need to vent periodic doggie tensions. . . . A pacifier if you will!

Dental caries, as they affect the teeth of humans, are virtually unknown in dogs; but tartar (calculus) accumulates on the teeth of dogs, particularly at the gum line, more rapidly than on the teeth of humans. These accumulations, if not removed, bring irritation and then infection, which erode the tooth enamel and ultimately destroy the teeth at the roots. It is important that you take your dog to your local veterinarian for periodic dental examinations.

Tooth and jaw development will normally continue until the dog is more than a year old—but sometimes much longer, depending upon the dog, its chewing exercise, rate of calcium utilization and many other factors, known and unknown, which affect the development of individual dogs. Diseases, like distemper for example, may sometimes arrest development of the teeth and jaws, which may resume months or even years later.

HARD PALATE

SOFT PALATE

ESOPHAGUS

VOCAL CORDS

EPIGLOTTIS

TONGUE

The owner should inspect the dog's mouth regularly to check that all is well.

This is why dogs, especially puppies and young dogs, will often destroy valuable property when their chewing instinct is not diverted from their owners' possessions, particularly during the widely varying critical period for young dogs. Saving your possessions from destruction, assuring proper development of teeth and jaws, providing for "interim" tooth cleaning and gum massage, and channeling doggie tensions into a non-destructive outlet are, therefore, all dependent upon the dog's having something suitable for chewing readily available when his instinct tells him to chew. If your purposes, and those of your dog, are to be accomplished, what you provide for chewing must be desirable from the doggie viewpoint, have the necessary functional qualities, and, above all, be safe.

It is very important that dogs be prohibited from chewing on anything they can break or indigestible things from which they can bite sizeable chunks. Sharp pieces, such as those from a bone which can be broken by a dog, may pierce the intestinal wall and kill. Indigestible things which can be bitten off in chunks, such as toys made of rubber compound or cheap plastic, may cause an intestinal stoppage; if not regurgitated, they are certain to bring painful death unless surgery is promptly performed.

NATURAL CHEW BONES

Strong natural bones, such as 4- to 8-inch lengths of round shin bone from mature beef—either the kind you can get from your butcher or one of the varieties available commercially in pet stores—may serve your dog's teething needs, if his mouth is large enough to handle them.

You may be tempted to give your puppy a smaller bone and he may not be able to break it when you do, but puppies grow rapidly and the power of their jaws constantly increases until maturity. This means that a growing dog may break one of

excessive chewing on animal bones. Contrary to popular belief, knuckle bones that can be chewed up and swallowed by the dog provide little, if any, useable calcium or other nutrient. They do, however, disturb the digestion of most dogs and might cause them to vomit the nourishing food they really need.

the smaller bones at any time, swallow the pieces and die painfully before you realize what is wrong.

All hard natural bones are highly abrasive. If your dog is an avid chewer, natural bones may wear away his teeth prematurely; hence, they then should be taken away from your dog when the teething purposes have been served. The badly worn, and usually painful, teeth of many mature dogs can be traced to

Rawhide treats are enjoyed by dogs. Owners should be wary since rawhide can tear off in large pieces and lodge in the dog's throat or cause intestinal blockage.

RAWHIDE CHEWS

The most popular material from which dog chews are made is the hide from cows, horses, and other animals. Most of these chews are made in foreign countries where the quality of the hide is not good enough for making leather. These foreign hides may contain lead, antibiotics, arsenic, or insecticides which might be detrimental to the health of your dog . . . or even your children. It is not impossible that a small child will start chewing on a piece of rawhide meant for the dog! Rawhide chews do not serve the primary chewing functions very well. They are also a bit messy when wet from mouthing, and most dogs chew them up rather rapidly. They have been considered safe for dogs until recently.

Rawhide is flavorful to dogs. They like it. Currently, some veterinarians have been attributing cases of acute constipation to large pieces of incompletely digested rawhide in the intestine. Basically it is good for them to chew on, but dogs think rawhide is food. They do not play with it nor do they use it as a pacifier to relieve doggie tension. They eat it as they would any other food. This is dangerous, for the hide is very difficult for dogs to digest and swallow, and many dogs choke on large particles of rawhide that become stuck in their throats. *Before you offer your dog rawhide chews, consult your veterinarian.* Vets have a lot of experience with canine chewing devices; ask them what they recommend.

Annealed nylon and polyurethane chew toys are recommended by veterinarians as proven-safe and effective canine chew devices.

NYLON CHEW DEVICES

The nylon bones, especially those with natural meat and bone flavor added, are probably the most complete, safe, and economical answer to the chewing need. Dogs cannot break them nor bite off sizeable chunks; hence, they are completely safe. And being longer lasting than other things offered for the purpose, they are very economical.

Hard chewing raises little bristle-like projections on the surface of the nylon bones to provide effective interim tooth

The Nylafloss® cannot cure tooth decay, but it is an optimum decay-prevention device. Make your dog's playtime a healthy time and invest in your pet's future.

cleaning and vigorous gum massage, much in the same way your toothbrush does it for you. The little projections are raked off and swallowed in the form of thin shavings, but the chemistry of the nylon is such that they break down in the stomach fluids and pass through without effect.

The toughness of the nylon provides the strong chewing resistance needed for important jaw exercise and effective help for the teething functions; however, there is no tooth wear because nylon is non-abrasive. Being inert, nylon does not support the growth of microorganisms, and it can be washed in soap and water or sterilized by boiling or in an autoclave.

There are a great variety of Nylabone® products available that veterinarians recommend as safe and healthy for your dog or puppy to chew on. These Nylabone® Pooch Pacifiers® usually don't splinter, chip, or break off in large chunks; instead, they are frizzled by the dog's chewing action, and this creates a toothbrush-like surface that cleanses the teeth and massages the gums. At the same time, these hard-nylon therapeutic devices channel doggie tension and chewing frustation into constructive rather than destructive behavior. The original nylon bone (Nylabone®) is not a toy and dogs use it only when in need of pacification. Keeping a bone in each of your dog's recreation rooms is the best method of providing the requisite pacification. Unfortunately, many nylon chew products have been copied. These inferior quality copies are sold in supermarkets and other chain stores. The really good products are sold only through veterinarians, pet shops, grooming salons and places where the sales people really know something about dogs. The good products have the flavor impregnated *into* the bone. This makes the taste last longer. The smell is undetectable to humans. The artificial bones which have a strong odor are poor-quality bones with the odor sprayed on to impress the dog owner (not the dog)! These heavily scented dog toys may impart the odor to your carpets or furniture if an odor-sprayed bone lies there wet from a dog's chewing on it.

revolutionary product that is designed to save dogs teeth and keep them healthy. Even though your dogs won't believe you, Nylafloss® is not a toy but rather a most effective agent in removing destructive plaque

Food particles can be deposited between the teeth, where they can be difficult to remove. Many chew products cannot work to remove these decaying food pieces. For this reason, the Nylafloss® dental device is recommended by professionals as it is the only available mechanism to clean between the dog's teeth.

FLOSS OR LOSS!

Most dentists relay that brushing daily is just not enough. In order to prevent unnecessary tooth loss, flossing is essential. For dogs, human dental floss is not the answer—however, canine dental devices are available. The Nylafloss® is a

between the teeth and *beneath* the gum line where gum disease begins. Gentle tugging is all that is necessary to activate the Nylafloss®. These 100% inert nylon products are guaranteed to outlast rawhide chews by ten times and are available for sale at all pet shops.

Preventive Dental Care

THE IMPORTANCE OF PREVENTION

In order to get to the root of canine dentistry problems, it is important for owners to realize that no less than 75% of all canine dental health problems, serious enough to require a vet's assistance, and nearly 98% of all canine teeth lost are attributable to periodontal disease.

A dog's teeth showing moderate calculus build-up. The moderate calculus build-up on this dog's teeth reflects a certain neglect by the owner. Providing a safe chew item like the Gumabone® can save your dog's teeth.

Periodontal disease not only mars the teeth but also the gums and other buccal tissue in the mouth. Severe cases of periodontal disease involve resultant bacterial toxins which are absorbed into the blood stream and cause permanent damage to the heart and kidneys. In the infected mouth, teeth are loosened; tartar, unsightly and bad smelling, accumulates heavily; and the dog experiences a complete loss of appetite. Long-standing periodontitis can also manifest itself in simple symptoms such as diarrhea and vomiting.

Periodontal disease deserves the attention of every dog owner—a dog's teeth are extremely important to his ongoing health. The accumulation of plaque, food matter mixed with saliva attaching itself to the tooth surface, is a sure sign of potential bacteria build-up. As toxic material gathers, the bone surrounding the teeth erodes. If plaque and calculus continue to reside without attention, bacteria-fighting cells will form residual pus at the root of the teeth, dividing the gum from the tooth. The debris is toxic and actually kills the buccal tissue. This is a most undesirable situation, as hardened dental calculus is one of the most direct causative agents of periodontitis.

In actuality, the disease is a result of a number of contributing factors. Old age, a diet comprised solely of soft or semi-soft foods, dental tartar, constant chewing of hair and even coprophagy (the eating of stool) are among the most common contributors.

Just as regular dental visits and brushing are necessary for humans, regular hygienic care and veterinary check-ups can help control tooth problems in canines. Involved and expensive routines can be performed on the affected, neglected mouth and teeth if decay has begun eroding the enamel and infecting the gums. Cleaning, polishing, and scaling are routine to remove calculus build-up.

Owners must claim responsibility for their dog's health, and tooth care is no small aspect of the care required. Daily brushing with a salt/baking soda solution is the best answer, but many owners find this tedious or just too difficult to perform. The simpler and more proven effective way to avoid, reduce, and fight periodontal disease and calculus build-up is giving the dog regular access to a thermoplastic polymer chew device. The Gumabone® products are the only scientifically proven line that offers the desired protection from calculus and tartar build-up.

CANINE DENTAL BREAKTHROUGH

The independent research of Dr. Andrew Duke, D.V.M., reveals that 70% of the dogs that regularly use Gumabone® experience a reduction of calculus build-up. This find is a breakthrough for the dog world, since the Gumabone® has already resided in the toy boxes

Regular use of the Gumabone® chew products can significantly reduce plaque build-up.

of many dogs as their favorite play item. Little did owners know previously that their dogs were gaining entertainment and unparalleled dental treatment at the same time. Dr. Duke writes: "There is little debate left that dental calculus is an excellent

Teeth of an infected dog showing little to no plaque accumulation after professional cleaning.

indicator of periodontal health in the dog, just as it is in humans. "Calculus does not cause gingivitis and periodontitis, but the plaque and bacteria that cause periodontitis are responsible for the mineral precipitation we know as 'calculus.' All veterinarians who have made a study of dogs' oral health have noticed the middle aged dog who actively chews with excellent gingival health. Many of these dogs that chew hard substances regularly wear the cusps down and even may expose the pulp cavity faster than secondary dentin can be formed. Often these "excellent chewers" are presented with slab fractures of the premolars or apical abcesses.

"The challenge then becomes to find a substance which is effective in removing calculus and plaque but does not wear the enamel excessively. In an attempt to duplicate the chewstuffs enjoyed by dogs in the wild, researchers have used bovine tracheas to demonstrate the inhibition of plaque and gingivitis. Very little else has been done in veterinary medicine

The clean healthy teeth that are desired in dogs should inspire owners to work towards better dental hygiene.

Plaque is formed by the food debris and bacterial deposits left on teeth. Due to the high carbon dioxide and pH levels in the mouth, minerals precipitate quickly on the plaque to form calculus.

to establish a scientific basis for evaluating chewstuffs.

"In the human field it is generally accepted (incorrectly) that fibrous foodstuffs and diet have no effect on oral health. This is a moot point since the practice of brushing is by far a more efficient technique of preventing plaque accumulation, calculus and periodontal disease. Studies in human subjects failed to find any benefits in eating apples, raw carrots, etc. If people are not allowed to brush, it is difficult to conduct clinical trials of more than one week.

"The increased awareness of animals' dental health of recent years has resulted in most veterinary practitioners' recommending some kind of chewstuff to their dog owners. To meet this market demand, there has been a stampede into the market by vendors ready to promote their products. The

Canine tooth brushes are designed to allow access to the most hard-to-reach places in the canine mouth.

veterinarian is furnished no scientific data, but is asked to promote rawhide, bounce, and squeaky toys. How would our human colleagues handle this situation? Can Listerine® say that it prevents colds, but not support the claim? Can "Tartar Control Crest®" or "Colgate Tartar Control Formula®" be sold if it is not proven that it does in fact reduce tartar? Of course not.

"To this end, the following study was made.

"*Method:* Twenty dogs of different breeds and age were selected from a veterinary

In cases of bad neglect, scaling a dog's teeth can help to save or salvage affected teeth. Your veterinarian will perform this procedure.

CUMULATIVE CALCULUS INDEX SCORES

Dog	Without Gumabone®	With Gumabone®	Difference
1.	20	9	11
2.	19	23	- 4
3.	49	26	23
4.	21	15	6
5.	34	11	23
6.	36	21	15
7.	44	31	13
8.	25	25	0
9.	34	28	6
10.	44	23	21
11.	22	15	7
12.	23	33	-10
13.	26	23	3
14.	22	14	8
15.	20	20	0
16.	23	13	10
17.	24	14	10
18.	24	17	7
19.	24	31	-7
20.	15	30	-15

As supported by Dr. Duke's study on reducing calculus build-up, the effectiveness of a chewing device can be measured by assigning numerical values to the accumulation when the Gumabone® device is used and not used. Seventy percent of dogs chewing Gumabone® (14 out of 20 dogs) showed a reduction in calculus build-up.

practice's clientele. Although most were from multiple pet households, none were colony dogs. The owners were asked if they would allow their dogs to be anesthetized for two prophylactic cleanings which included root planing, polishing, and gingival debridement necessary to insure good oral hygiene.

"The dogs were divided into two groups of 10. Their teeth were cleaned and their calculus index converted to 0. One group was allowed only their normal dry commercial dog ration for 30 days. The other was allowed to have free choice access to Gumabone® products of the appropriate size.

"After 30 days, photoslides were made of the upper 3rd premolar, upper 4th premolar, and the lower 4th premolar on both sides of the dog's mouth. The dogs were again subjected to a prophylactic cleaning and the group reversed. After the second 30 days, photoslides were again made. A total of six teeth in each mouth were evaluated on each dog. This was 80 slides representing 240 teeth."

Fourteen out of 20 dogs (or 70%) experienced a reduction in calculus build-up by regularly using the Gumabone® product. These products are available in a variety of sizes (for different size dogs) and designed in interesting shapes: bones, balls,

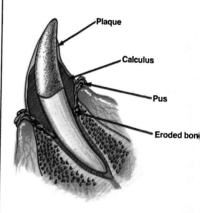

Comparative look at healthy gums (above) and affected gums (below) *in a dog's mouth. Instinctively dogs need to massage their gums—and the Gumabone® can satisfy this doggie craving.*

knots and rings (and even a tug toy). The entertainment value of the Gumabone® products is but an added advantage to the fighting of tooth decay and periodontitis. The products are ham-flavored and made of a thermoplastic polymer that is designed to outlast by ten times any rawhide, rubber or vinyl chew product, none of which can promise the proven benefit of the Gumabone®.

If your dog is able to chew apart a Gumabone®, it is probable that you provided him with a bone that is too small for him. Replace it with a larger one and the problem should not re-materialize. Economically, the Gumabone® is a smart choice, even without comparing it to the cost of extensive dental care.

Of course, nothing can *substitute* for periodic professional attention to your dog's teeth and gums, no more than your toothbrush can replace your dentist. Have your dog's teeth cleaned by your veterinarian at least once a year—twice a year is better—and he will be healthier, happier, and a far more pleasant companion.

Gumabones® are available through veterinarians and pet shops.

PERPETUAL WHELPING CHART

Bred—Jan.   1 2 3 4 5 6 7 8 9 10 11 12 13 14 15 16 17 18 19 20 21 22 23 24 25 26 27 28 29 30 31
Due—March   5 6 7 8 9 10 11 12 13 14 15 16 17 18 19 20 21 22 23 24 25 26 27 28 29 30 31   **April** 1 2 3 4

Bred—Feb.   1 2 3 4 5 6 7 8 9 10 11 12 13 14 15 16 17 18 19 20 21 22 23 24 25 26 27 28
Due—April   5 6 7 8 9 10 11 12 13 14 15 16 17 18 19 20 21 22 23 24 25 26 27 28 29 30   **May** 1 2

Bred—Mar.   1 2 3 4 5 6 7 8 9 10 11 12 13 14 15 16 17 18 19 20 21 22 23 24 25 26 27 28 29 30 31
Due—May   3 4 5 6 7 8 9 10 11 12 13 14 15 16 17 18 19 20 21 22 23 24 25 26 27 28 29 30 31   **June** 1 2

Bred—Apr.   1 2 3 4 5 6 7 8 9 10 11 12 13 14 15 16 17 18 19 20 21 22 23 24 25 26 27 28 29 30
Due—June   3 4 5 6 7 8 9 10 11 12 13 14 15 16 17 18 19 20 21 22 23 24 25 26 27 28 29 30   **July** 1 2

Bred—May   1 2 3 4 5 6 7 8 9 10 11 12 13 14 15 16 17 18 19 20 21 22 23 24 25 26 27 28 29 30 31
Due—July   3 4 5 6 7 8 9 10 11 12 13 14 15 16 17 18 19 20 21 22 23 24 25 26 27 28 29 30 31   **August** 1 2

Bred—June   1 2 3 4 5 6 7 8 9 10 11 12 13 14 15 16 17 18 19 20 21 22 23 24 25 26 27 28 29 30
Due—August   3 4 5 6 7 8 9 10 11 12 13 14 15 16 17 18 19 20 21 22 23 24 25 26 27 28 29 30   **Sept.** 1

Bred—July   1 2 3 4 5 6 7 8 9 10 11 12 13 14 15 16 17 18 19 20 21 22 23 24 25 26 27 28 29 30 31
Due—September   2 3 4 5 6 7 8 9 10 11 12 13 14 15 16 17 18 19 20 21 22 23 24 25 26 27 28 29 30   **Oct.** 1 2

Bred—Aug.   1 2 3 4 5 6 7 8 9 10 11 12 13 14 15 16 17 18 19 20 21 22 23 24 25 26 27 28 29 30 31
Due—October   3 4 5 6 7 8 9 10 11 12 13 14 15 16 17 18 19 20 21 22 23 24 25 26 27 28 29 30 31   **Nov.** 1 2

Bred—Sept.   1 2 3 4 5 6 7 8 9 10 11 12 13 14 15 16 17 18 19 20 21 22 23 24 25 26 27 28 29 30
Due—November   3 4 5 6 7 8 9 10 11 12 13 14 15 16 17 18 19 20 21 22 23 24 25 26 27 28 29 30   **Dec.** 1 2

Bred—Oct.   1 2 3 4 5 6 7 8 9 10 11 12 13 14 15 16 17 18 19 20 21 22 23 24 25 26 27 28 29 30 31
Due—December   3 4 5 6 7 8 9 10 11 12 13 14 15 16 17 18 19 20 21 22 23 24 25 26 27 28 29 30 31   **Jan.** 1 2

Bred—Nov.   1 2 3 4 5 6 7 8 9 10 11 12 13 14 15 16 17 18 19 20 21 22 23 24 25 26 27 28 29 30
Due—January   3 4 5 6 7 8 9 10 11 12 13 14 15 16 17 18 19 20 21 22 23 24 25 26 27 28 29 30 31   **Feb.** 1

Bred—Dec.   1 2 3 4 5 6 7 8 9 10 11 12 13 14 15 16 17 18 19 20 21 22 23 24 25 26 27 28 29 30 31
Due—February   2 3 4 5 6 7 8 9 10 11 12 13 14 15 16 17 18 19 20 21 22 23 24 25 26 27 28   **March** 1 2 3 4

Breeding

As the owner of a purebred dog, you may have considered breeding your pet at one time or another. If your dog is a beloved family pet, and not a show dog, you should *not* breed your dog. Breeding is not a hobby for pet owners, but rather a demanding, complicated vocation that is not to be dabbled with. Many people have thought of breeding as an easy-money opportunity: buy two dogs and let them do the work. The rule of thumb is: if you're making money by breeding dogs, you're doing something wrong!

Consider the time and money involved just to get your bitch into breeding condition and then to sustain her throughout pregnancy and afterwards while she tends her young. You will be obligated to house, feed, groom, and housebreak the puppies until good homes can be found for them; and, lest we forget, there will be periodic trips to the vet for check-ups, wormings, and inoculations. Common sense should tell you that it is indeed cruel to bring unwanted or unplanned puppies into an already crowded canine world; only negligent pet owners allow this to happen. Recognizing the number of dogs, purebred and mixed breeds, pet-, show- and breeding-quality, that are put to sleep annually, responsible breeders require that all pet animals be neutered. This condition most often is incorporated into the selling contract. The motives of good breeders are clear: avoid the manufacturing and mass-producing of average and below-average dogs; control the overblown canine population; concentrate on the improvement of purebred bloodlines. Breeding is a noble calling and unless you can improve the breed, you should not consider breeding your animal. Despite all of the obvious virtues of breeding texts, no book could ever prepare a person for breeding. What a heart-breaking and tragic experience to lose an entire litter because a good-intentioned pet owner wasn't aware of potential genetic complications, didn't recognize a breech birth, or couldn't identify the signals of a struggling bitch! Possibly the dam could be lost as well!

Before you take any step towards mating your bitch, think carefully about why you want her to give birth to a litter of puppies. If you feel she will be deprived in some way if she is not bred, if you think your children will learn from the experience, if you have the mistaken notion that you will make money from this great undertaking, think again. A dog can lead a perfectly happy, healthy, normal life without having been mated; in fact, spaying a female and neutering a male helps them become better, longer-lived pets, as they are not

Breeding

so anxious to search for a mate in an effort to relieve their sexual tensions and have a diminished risk of cancer. As for giving the children a lesson in sex education, this is hardly a valid reason for breeding your dog. And on an economic level, it takes not only years of hard work (researching pedigrees and bloodlines, studying genetics, among other things), but it takes plenty of capital (money, equipment, facilities) to make a decent profit from dog breeding.

Why most dedicated breeders are lucky just to break even. If you have only a casual interest in dog breeding, it is best to leave this pastime to those who are more experienced in such matters, those who consider it a serious hobby and a real vocation. If you have bought a breeder– or show-quality canine, one that may be capable of producing champions, and if you are just starting out with this breeding venture, seek advice from the seller of your dog, from

Breeding dogs requires more than book knowledge. In dogs, breech presentation is not uncommon and the breeder must be prepared to handle this situation and guide the puppy so that neither the pup nor the bitch is injured.

other veteran breeders, and from your veterinarian before you begin.

The following sections on reproduction are intended for academic value only. This is not a "How-to" chapter on breeding, nor a step-by-step approach for the novice for getting started. Hopefully the reader will understand the depth and complexity of breeding as well as the expected ethical and moral obligations of persons who choose to do so—and never attempt it.

THE FEMALE "IN SEASON"

A bitch may come into season (also known as "heat" or estrus) once or several times a year, depending on the particular breed and the individual dog. Her first seasonal period, that is to say, the time when she is capable of being fertilized by a male dog, may occur as early as six months with some breeds. If you own a female and your intention is *not* to breed her, by all means discuss with the vet the possibility of having her spayed: this means before she

Ideally the puppy will be delivered in the normal, head-first position.

Breeding

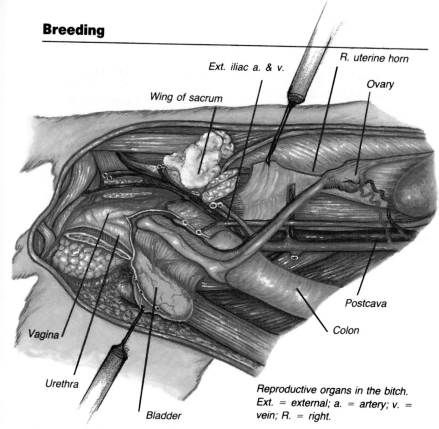

Reproductive organs in the bitch.
Ext. = external; a. = artery; v. = vein; R. = right.

Labels: Ext. iliac a. & v.; R. uterine horn; Ovary; Wing of sacrum; Postcava; Colon; Vagina; Urethra; Bladder

The reproductive system of the female dog consists of a highly specialized system of organs situated to the rear of the animal.

reaches sexual maturity.

The first sign of the female's being in season is a thin red discharge, which may increase for about a week; it then changes color to a thin yellowish stain, which lasts about another week. Simultaneously, there is a swelling of the vulva, the exterior portion of the female's reproductive tract; the soft, flabby vulva indicates her readiness to mate. Around this second week or so ovulation

occurs, and this is the crucial period for her to be bred, if this is what you have in mind for her. It is during this middle phase of the heat cycle when conception can take place. Just remember that there is great variation from bitch to bitch with regard to how often they come into heat, how long the heat cycles last, how long the period of ovulation lasts, and how much time elapses between heat cycles. Generally, after the third week of heat, the vulval swelling decreases and the estrus period ceases for several months.

It should be mentioned that the female will probably lose her puppy coat, or at least shed part of it, about three months after she has come into season. This is the time when her puppies would have been weaned, had she been mated, and females generally drop coat at this time.

With female dogs, there are few, if any, behavioral changes during estrus. A bitch may dart out of an open door to greet all available male dogs that show an interest in her, and she may occasionally raise her tail and assume a mating stance, particularly if you pet her lower back; but these signs are not as dramatic as those of the sexually mature male. He himself does

Each egg within the female is surrounded by a wall that normally takes many sperm to penetrate. In this way, it is more likely that only the strongest sperm will fertilize the egg. A fertile female in season usually has a number of eggs, known as gametes.

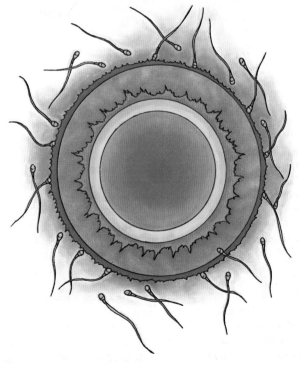

not experience heat cycles; rather, he is attracted to the female during all phases of her seasonal period. He usually becomes more aggressive and tends to fight with other males, especially over females in heat. He tends to mark his territory with urine to attract females and at the same time to warn other competitive males. It is not uncommon to see him mount various objects, and people, in an effort to satisfy his mature sexual urges.

If you are a homeowner and you have an absolutely climb-proof and dig-proof run within your yard, it may be safe to leave your bitch in season there. But then again it may not be a wise idea, as there have been cases of males mating with females right through chain-link fencing! Just to be on the safe side, shut her indoors during her heat periods and don't let her outdoors until you are certain the estrus period is over. Never leave a bitch in heat outdoors, unsupervised, even for a minute so that she can defecate or urinate. If you want to prevent the neighborhood dogs from hanging around your doorstep, as they inevitably will do when they discover your female is in season, take her some distance away from the house before you let her do her business. Otherwise, these canine suitors will be attracted to her by the

arousing odor of her urine, and they will know instinctively that she isn't far from her scented "calling card." If you need to walk your bitch, take her in the car to a nearby park or field for a chance to stretch her legs. Remember that after about three weeks, and this varies from dog to dog, you can let her outdoors again with no worry that she can have puppies until the next heat period.

If you are seriously considering breeding your dog, first talk to as many experienced breeders as possible and read up on the subject in specific books and articles. Only when you are fully aware of the demands and responsibilities of breeding should you make your final decision. It must be stated here that there is no shortage of fine dogs in need of good homes, nor is there likely to be in the foreseeable future. So, if your object in breeding is merely to produce more dogs, you are strongly encouraged to reconsider your objective.

WHEN TO BREED

It is usually best to breed a bitch when she comes into her second or third season. Plan in advance the time of year which is best for you, taking into account your own schedule of activities (vacations, business trips, social engagements, and so on). Make sure you will be able to set aside plenty of time to assist with whelping of the newborn pups and caring for the dam and her litter for the next few weeks. At

The male reproductive system includes the penis and testicles. When not excited, the penis is withdrawn into the dog's body.

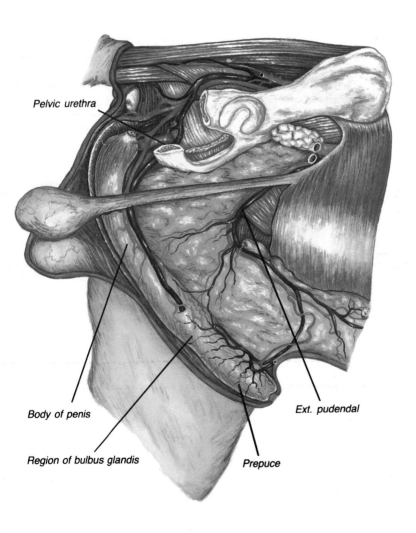

Pelvic urethra

Body of penis

Region of bulbus glandis

Ext. pudendal

Prepuce

the very least, it probably will take an hour or so each day just to feed and clean up after the brood—but undoubtedly you will find it takes much longer if you stop to admire and play with the youngsters periodically! Refrain from selling the litter until it is at least six weeks old, keeping in mind that a litter of pups takes up a fair amount of space by then. It will be your responsibility to provide for them until they have been weaned from their mother, properly socialized, housebroken, and ready to go to new homes (unless you plan to keep them all). Hopefully, as strongly recommended, you will have already lined up buyers for the pups in advance of their arrival into this world.

CHOOSING THE STUD

You can plan to breed your female about six-and-one-half months after the start of her last season, although a variation of a month or two either way is not unusual. Do some research into the various bloodlines within your breed and then choose a stud dog and make arrangements well in advance. If you are breeding for show stock, which will command higher prices than pet-quality animals, a mate should be chosen very carefully. He should complement any deficiencies (bad traits) that your female may have, and he should have a good show record

or be the sire of show winners, if he is old enough to have proven himself. If possible, the bitch and stud should have several ancestors in common within the last two or three generations, as such combinations have been known, generally, to "click" best.

The owner of a stud dog usually charges a stud fee for use of the animal's services. This does not always guarantee a litter, but if she fails to conceive, chances are you may be able to breed your female to that stud again. In some instances the owner of the stud will agree to take a "first pick of the litter" in place of a fee. You should, of course, settle all details beforehand, including the possibility of a single puppy surviving, deciding the age at which the pup is to be taken, and so forth.

If you plan to raise a litter that will be sold exclusively as pets, and if you merely plan to make use of an available male (not a top stud dog), the most important selection point involves temperament. Make sure the dog is friendly, as well as healthy, because a bad disposition can be passed on to his puppies—and this is the worst of all traits in a dog destined to be a pet. If you are breeding pet-quality dogs, a "stud fee puppy," not necessarily the choice of the litter, is the usual payment. Don't

Whelping box prepared with "pig rails," bars on either side of the box to prevent the bitch from rolling on the puppies.

breed indiscriminately; be sure you will be able to find good homes for each of the pups.

PREPARATION FOR BREEDING

Before you breed your female, make sure she is in good health. She should be neither too thin nor too fat. Any skin disease *must* be cured first so that it is not passed on to the puppies. If she has worms, she should be wormed before being bred or within three weeks after the mating. It is generally considered a good idea to revaccinate her against distemper and hepatitis before the puppies are born.

The female will probably be ready to breed twelve days after the first colored discharge appears. You can usually make arrangements to board her with the owner of the stud for a few days, to insure her being there at the proper time; or you can take her to be mated and bring her home the same day if you live near enough to the stud's owner. If the bitch still appears receptive she may be bred again two days later, just to make certain the mating was successful. However, some females never show signs of willingness, so it helps to have an experienced breeder on hand. In fact, you both may have to assist with the mating by holding the animals against each other to ensure the "tie" is not broken, that is, to make certain copulation takes place.

Usually the second day after the discharge changes color is the proper time to mate the bitch, and she may be bred for about three days following this time. For an additional week or so, she may have some discharge and attract other dogs by her odor; but she should not be bred. Once she has been bred, keep her far from all other male dogs, as they have the capacity to impregnate her again and sire some of her puppies. This could prove disastrous with purebred puppies.

THE FEMALE IN WHELP

You can expect the puppies nine weeks from the day of the mating, although sixty-one days is as common as sixty-three. Gestation, that period when the pups are developing inside their mother, varies among individual bitches. During this time the female should receive normal care and exercise. If she was overweight at the start, don't increase her food right away; excess weight at whelping time can be a problem with some dogs. If she is on the thin side, however, supplement her meal or meals with a portion of milk and biscuit at noontime. This will help build her up and put weight on her.

You may want to add a mineral and vitamin supplement to her diet, on the advice of your veterinarian, since she will need an extra supply not only for herself but for the puppies growing inside her. As the mother's appetite increases, feed her more. During the last two weeks of pregnancy, the pups grow enormously and the mother will have little room for food and less of an appetite. She should be tempted with meat, liver, and milk, however.

As the female in whelp grows heavier, cut out violent exercise and jumping from her usual routine. Although a dog used to such activities will often play with the children or run around voluntarily, restrain her for her own sake.

A sign that whelping is imminent is the loss of hair around her breasts. This is nature's way of "clearing a path" so that the puppies will be able to find their source of nourishment. As parturition draws near, the breasts will have swelled with milk and the nipples will have enlarged and darkened to a rosy pink. If the hair in the breast region does not shed for some reason, you can easily cut it short with a pair of scissors or comb it out so that it does not mat and become a hindrance to the suckling pups later on.

PREPARING FOR THE PUPPIES

Prepare a whelping box a few days before the puppies are due, and allow the mother to sleep there overnight or to spend some time in it during the day to become accustomed to it. This way she is less likely to try to have her pups under the front porch or in the middle of your bed. A variety of places will serve, such as the corner of your cellar or garage (provided these

Each puppy is delivered in a separate membranous sac. This sac must be removed by the bitch without delay—if not, the breeder must come immediately to the assistance of the pup.

places are warm and dry). An unused room, such as a dimly lit spare bedroom, can also serve as the place for delivery. If the weather is warm, a large outdoor dog house will do, as long as it is well protected from rain, drafts, and the cold—and enclosed by fencing or a run. A whelping box serves to separate mother and puppies from visitors and other distractions. The walls should be high enough to restrain the puppies yet low enough to allow the mother to take a short respite from her brood after she has fed them. Four feet square is minimum size (for most dogs) and six-to-eight-inch high walls will keep the pups in until they begin to climb; then side walls should be built up so that the young ones cannot wander away from their nest. As the puppies

grow, they really need more room anyway, so double the space with a very low partition down the middle of the box, and soon you will find them naturally housebreaking themselves. Puppies rarely relieve themselves where they sleep. Layers of newspapers spread over the whole area will make excellent bedding and be absorbent enough to keep the surface warm and dry. These should be removed daily and replaced with another thick layer. An old quilt or washable blanket makes better footing for the nursing puppies than slippery newspaper during the first week; this is also softer for the mother to lie on.

Be prepared for the actual whelping several days in advance. Usually the mother will

Breeding

tear up papers, refuse food, and become restless. These may be false alarms; the real test is her temperature, which will drop to below 100°F (38°C) about twelve hours before whelping. Take her temperature with a rectal thermometer, morning and evening, and usher her to her whelping box when her temperature goes down. Keep a close watch on her and make sure she stays safely indoors (or outdoors in a safe enclosure); if she is let outside, unleashed, or allowed to roam freely, she could wander off and start to go into labor. It is possible that she could whelp anywhere, and this could be unfortunate if she needs your assistance.

WHELPING

Usually little help is needed from you, but it is wise to stay close to be sure that the mother's lack of experience (if this is her first time) does not cause an unnecessary complication. Be ready to help when the first puppy arrives, for it could smother if she does not break the amniotic membrane enclosing it. She should tear open the sac and start licking the puppy, drying and stimulating it. Check to see that all fluids have been cleared from the pup's nostrils and mouth after the mother has licked her youngster clean; otherwise the pup may have difficulty breathing. If the

mother fails to tear open the sac and stimulate the newborn's breathing, you can do this yourself by tearing the sack with your hands and then gently rubbing the infant with a soft, rough towel. The afterbirth attached to the puppy by the long umbilical cord, should follow the birth of each puppy. Watch to be sure that each afterbirth is expelled, for the retention of this material can cause infection. In her instinct for cleanliness the mother will probably eat the afterbirth after severing the umbilical cord. One or two meals of this will not hurt her; they stimulate her milk supply, as well as labor, for remaining pups. However, eating too many afterbirths can make her lose appetite for the food she needs to feed her pups and regain her strength. So remove the rest of them, along with the wet newspapers, and keep the box dry and clean.

If the mother does not bite the cord or bites it too close to the puppy's body, take over the job to prevent an umbilical hernia. Tearing is recommended, but you can cut the cord, about two inches from the body, with a sawing motion with scissors that have been sterilized in alcohol. Then dip the end of the cut cord in a shallow dish of iodine; the cord will dry up and fall off in a few days.

The puppies should follow

each other at intervals of not more than half an hour. If more time goes past and you are sure there are still pups to come, taking the mother for a brisk walk outside may start labor again. If she is actively straining without producing a puppy, the youngster may be presented backward, a so-called "breech" birth. Careful assistance with a well-lubricated finger to feel for the puppy or to ease it back may help, but never attempt to pull it out by force. This could cause serious damage, so seek the services of an expert—your veterinarian or an experienced breeder.

Even the best planned breeding can bear unexpected problems and complications. Therefore, do not rely solely on textbook knowledge of breeding and genetics. Experienced breeders and veterinarians will generally lend their words of wisdom—take full advantage of their generosity. Mere trial and error is no basis for any responsible breeding program.

If *anything* seems wrong during labor or parturition, waste no time in calling your veterinarian, who will examine the bitch and, if necessary, give her hormones to stimulate the birth of the remaining puppies. You may want his experience in whelping the litter even if all goes well. He will probably prefer to have the puppies born at his

Newborn pups are very susceptible to chills, so the breeder must dry the puppy off thoroughly and place it in a temperature-controlled puppy box.

hospital rather than getting up in the middle of the night to come to your home. The mother would, no doubt, prefer to stay at home; but you can be sure she will get the best of care in a veterinary hospital. If the puppies are born at home, and all goes as it should, watch the mother carefully afterward. Within a day or two of the birth, it is wise to have the veterinarian check her and the pups to ensure that all is well.

Small bowls are helpful in the weaning process. Each pup should have its own bowl so that food intake can be carefully monitored.

Be sure each puppy finds a teat and starts nursing right away, as these first few meals supply colostral antibodies to help him fight disease. As soon as he is dry, hold each puppy to a nipple for a good meal without competition. Then he may join his littermates in the whelping box, out of his mother's way while she continues giving birth. Keep a supply of puppy formula on hand for emergency feedings or later weaning. An alternative formula of evaporated milk, corn syrup, and a little water with egg yolk can be warmed and fed if necessary. A pet nurser kit is also a good thing to have on hand; these are available at local pet shops. A supplementary feeding often helps weak pups

(those that may have difficulty nursing) over the hump. Keep track of birth weights and weekly readings thereafter; this will furnish an accurate record of the pups' growth and health, and the information will be valuable to your veterinarian.

RAISING THE PUPPIES

After all the puppies have been born, take the mother outside for a walk and drink of water, and then return her to take care of her brood. She will probably not want to stay away for more than a minute or two for the first few weeks. Be sure to keep water available at all times and feed her milk or broth frequently, as she needs nourishment to produce milk. Encourage her to eat, with her favorite foods, until she seeks them of her own accord. She will soon develop a ravenous appetite and should have at least two large meals a day, with dry food available in addition. Your veterinarian can guide you on the finer points of nutrition as they apply to nursing dams.

Prepare a warm place to put the puppies after they are born to keep them dry and to help them to a good start in life. An electric heating pad, heat lamp or hot water bottle covered with flannel can be placed in the bottom of a cardboard box and near the mother so that she can see her puppies. She will usually allow you to help her care for the youngsters, but don't take them out of her sight. Let her handle things if your interference seems to make her nervous.

Be sure that all the puppies are getting enough to eat. If the mother sits or stands instead of lying still to nurse, the probable cause is scratching from the puppies' nails. You can remedy this by clipping them, as you would the bitch's, with a pet nail clipper. Manicure scissors also do

furnished with a heating pad and/or heating lamp and some bedding material. Leave half the litter with the mother and the other half in the extra box, changing off at two-hour intervals at first. Later you may exchange them less frequently, leaving them all together except during the day. Try supplementary feedings, too. As soon as their eyes open, at about two weeks, they will lap from a small dish.

"Pooping" the puppies, or rubbing the bowels and genitals to stimulate elimination, may be necessary if the bitch doesn't tend to this herself.

for these tiny claws. Some breeders advise disposing of the smaller or weaker pups in a large litter, as the mother has trouble handling more than six or seven. You can help her out by preparing an extra puppy box or basket

WEANING THE PUPPIES

Normally the puppies should be completely weaned at five weeks, although you can start to feed them at three weeks. They will find it easier to lap semi-solid food than to drink milk at first, so mix baby cereal with whole or evaporated milk, warmed to body temperature, and offer it to the puppies in a saucer. Until they learn to lap it, it is best to feed one or two at a time because they are more likely to walk into it than to eat it. Hold the saucer at their chin level, and let them gather around, keeping paws off the dish. Cleaning with a damp sponge afterward prevents most of the cereal from sticking to the pups if the mother doesn't clean them up. Once they have gotten the idea, broth or babies' meat soup may be alternated with milk, and you can start them on finely chopped meat. At about four weeks, they will eat four meals a day and soon do without their mother entirely. Start them on canned dog food, or leave dry puppy food with them in a dish

for self-feeding. Don't leave the water dish with them all the time; at this age everything is a play toy and they will use it as a wading pool. They can drink all they need if it is offered several times a day, after meals. As the puppies grow up, the mother will go into their "pen" only to nurse them, first sitting up and then standing. To dry up her milk

All puppies are susceptible to worms. Deworming must begin at a very early age with the supervision of a professional.

Bottle-feeding may be necessary with particularly large litters or with a bitch who has become overly stressed or neglectful.

supply completely, keep the mother away for longer periods; after a few days of part-time nursing she can stay away for even longer periods, and then permanently. The little milk left will be resorbed by her body.

The puppies may be put outside during the day, unless it is too cold or rainy, as soon as their eyes are open. They will benefit from the sunlight. A rubber mat or newspapers underneath will protect them from cold or dampness. As they mature, the pups can be let out for longer intervals, although you must provide them with a shelter at night or in bad weather. By now, cleaning up after the

matured youngsters is a man-sized job, so put them out at least during the day and make your task easier. If you enclose them in a run or kennel, remember to clean it *daily*, as various parasites and other infectious organisms may be lurking if the quarters are kept dirty.

You can expect the pups to need at least one worming before they are ready to go to new homes. Before the pups are three weeks old, take a stool sample from each to your veterinarian. The vet can determine, by analyzing the stool, if any of the pups have worms—and if so, what kind of

Breeding

worms are present. If one puppy is infected, then all should be wormed as a preventive measure. Follow the veterinarian's advice; this also applies to vaccinations. You will want to vaccinate the pups at the earliest possible age. This way, the pups destined for new homes will be protected against some of the more debilitating canine diseases.

THE DECISION TO SPAY OR NEUTER

If you decide not to use your male or female for breeding, or if you are obligated to have the animal altered based on an agreement made between you and the seller, make the necessary arrangements with your veterinarian as soon as possible. The surgery involved for both males and females is relatively simple and painless: males will be castrated and females will have their ovaries and uterus removed. In both cases, the operation does not alter their personalities; you will, however, notice that males will be less likely to roam, to get into fights with other male dogs, and to mount objects and people.

Your veterinarian can best determine at what age neutering or spaying should be done. With a young female dog, the operation may be somewhat more involved, and as a result be more costly; however, in the long

The breeder must actively partake in cleaning the pup after feedings. Hands-on contact serves as the initial step in socialization—accustoming the pup to his human family.

PUPPY GROWTH AND BREEDER RESPONSIBILITY	
AGE	**REQUIRED CARE/EXPECTED DEVELOPMENT**
WEEKS 1–2	Helpless; dam must provide constant care; owner must ensure warmth and cleanliness; puppy nurses, crawls, needs stimulation for elimination; sleeps 90% of time.
WEEKS 3–4	Owner sustains optimum environment; puppy is alert, laps from bowl, takes first steps; defecates on its own; baby teeth emerge; barks, wags tail.
WEEKS 4–5	Ambles, growls, and bites; play and interaction increase; human contact limited but essential; learning begins.
WEEKS 5–6	Weaning; human socialization vital; pack order apparent; sex play; explores and sleeps less.
WEEKS 6–8	Two to three daily meals; puppy accustomed to human family; breeder initiates housetraining; first veterinary visit; wary of the unknown.

run you will be glad you made the decision to have this done for your pet. After a night or two at the veterinarian's or an animal hospital, your bitch can be safely returned to your home. Her stitches will heal in a short time, and when they are removed, you will hardly notice her souvenir scar of the routine operation. Once she has been spayed, she no longer will be capable of having a litter of puppies.

Check with your city or town or with the local humane society for special programs that are available for pet owners. In many municipalities you can have your pet altered for just a small fee; the low price is meant to encourage pet owners to take advantage of this important means of birth control for their dogs. Pet adoption agencies and other animal welfare organizations can house only so many animals at one time, given the money, space, and other resources they have available. This is why pet owners are urged to have their pets altered, so that puppies resulting from accidental breedings won't end up being put to sleep as so many others have that are lost, stray, unwanted, or abandoned.

Dogs and the Law

BY ANMARIE BARRIE

No matter where you live, there will be laws and ordinances restricting the ownership of pets—exotic and wild animals (such as monkeys, pythons, and ocelots) as well as the more traditionally kept domestics (such as dogs and cats). This chapter purports to investigate with brevity the laws which pertain to the ownership and keeping of the domestic canine. Like all other things, laws change and evolve over time, and vary from locale to locale. The information supplied in this chapter is meant as a general guideline for the dog owner. Every owner is strongly encouraged to contact his local authorities to keep abreast on new laws and amendments to existing laws so that he can be the most responsible owner possible.

BUYING AND SELLING

Certain specific laws apply to the purchasing and peddling of pooches. Laws in these areas grow ever more stringent, so the potential buyer and/or seller is well advised to be aware of the laws pertaining to his transactions where dogs are concerned. Dealers and breeders, in most instances, are treated differently from the average dog owner who is trying to sell his first litter. Regardless, a sales contract is in order, a written agreement outlining the various dimensions of the sale. Sales contracts may indicate the quality of the dog, i.e.,

the pet-quality, show-quality, breeder-quality; the sex of the dog; and the breed of the dog. In addition to these basic essentials, the specifics, as registered with the national kennel club, should be included, i.e., the names and registration numbers of the sire and dam; the litter registration number; addresses of all involved, etc. Warranties and conditions of the sale should also be expressly stated, and no implications or unexpressed conditions may apply. For instance, the return policy, the guaranteed pedigree of the dog, the health of the dog (including the possibility of congenital defects in later years) should all be addressed. Replacement warranties are also appropriate to include, should something happen to the purchased puppy. Should a given puppy (of intended show-quality) begin to exhibit faults disqualified in the breed standard, the buyer is able to return the dog. Commonly, if the seller is no longer in the business of selling dogs, the buyer is entitled to half of the agreed-upon price.

GENERAL GUIDELINES FOR DOG OWNERS

"Give to God what is God's, give to Caesar what is Caesar's" is a Gospel quote that has been used and manipulated since it was originally uttered two thousand years ago. The concept of paying taxes has never sat well with humans, nor does it sit well with dogs. Licenses are basically taxes on dogs, though as pet owners we need not stew over the unfairness of "yet another tax." The purpose of licensing dogs is a valid and important one. Licenses serve as a positive means of identifying an animal and afford an owner with a fair chance of regaining his dog if lost or stolen. Licenses also provide a dog additional consideration by authorities and even from strangers, who will respect the fact the owner of this dog cares enough to identify it and affix its ID to its collar.

Many owners resist the call to license their dogs on the premise that their dogs are house dogs or yard dogs, or never ever walk off their leashes. Nonetheless, accidents and mishaps occur regularly, and it's better to be safe than sorry (why not be safe and law-abiding!?). The threat of impoundment and the treatment which dogs receive as a matter of course from such authorities should be scare tactic enough to persuade an owner to license his dog.

The cost of licenses varies from place to place as well as from dog to dog. Licenses for assistance dogs, such as Seeing Eye dogs, hearing dogs, or any handicap-assistance dogs, may be substan-

Dogs and the Law

tially less than a regular dog. In some areas, assistance dogs receive their licenses gratis, or are covered by their training agency. Recognizing the growing problem of dog over-population, many towns and cities offer reduced license fees for spayed and neutered dogs.

Vaccinations for dogs deserve special mention. Depending on where you live, the vaccination for rabies may or may not be mandatory. In some places, this vaccination is optional. While the chances of your well-kept canine acquiring rabies today may be minuscule, the cases are not so isolated and unheard of that an owner can rest in ultimate confidence. Generally a vaccinated dog can avoid being

quarantined in the unfortunate event that it should bite a stranger or would-be assailant. The age for vaccination varies, but most usual is six months old. If a puppy is under the age of six months, it is advisable not to permit it to socialize with unknown dogs on the street. Keep in mind that vaccinations need to be kept updated for both rabies and other diseases.

Among the most common-sense concerns of current-day owners are leash laws. Responsible dog owners marvel with dismay over dogs which run the neighborhood without a collar, supervision, or their owner's concern. Caring dog proprietors are grateful for leash laws as it is the protection of the dog, as well as human passers-by, that is concerned. That a dog is under control at all times remains the premise of leash laws. Dogs that are given the "freedom" to wander the neighborhood or city block are likewise given the "right" to be impounded, snatched and/or injured. Fines are often issued against owners who do not abide by the leash laws of their community.

Running hand in hand, or paw in paw, with leash laws are muzzle ordinances. These laws require that a dog be muzzled at all times when it is in public. Although these laws are less commonplace than leash laws, they do exist in certain communities. Owners are advised to investigate if muzzle laws apply in their area.

Pooper-scooper laws are being enforced in more and more areas these days. "Curb Your Dog" signs have become as common as pedestrian crossings and "Yield signs." For the cleanliness of our communities, these kinds of laws are invented; in order to do our part as responsible dog owners and citizens, we must abide by these clean-up rules. While persons who live in the country have more gripes with these laws, city dwellers fully understand the need to observe these ordinances. Scoops are sold in pet shops, or you can employ simple plastic bags. It is assured that if you are the person walking behind the behind of a 250-pound pooch, you will be grateful for these laws. Some owners use brown paper sheets or newspapers (preferably yesterday's) to assist in the clean-up.

Anti-cruelty laws are geared towards the protection of animals on the whole, sparing dogs from potential, often unintentional, abuse. Laws such as these are sweeping the nations, as an increasing number of people become aware of deleterious situations arising for all animals. While active cruelty to an animal

evokes rage in any human being, there are more subtle displays of cruelty which these laws attempt to pinpoint—cruelty in the form of neglect and careless treatment. Persons who are found in violation of anti-cruelty laws are very often subject to fines. All citizens are encouraged to report any cases of cruelty which they witness or suspect to be happening. Commonly, ordinances prohibit the keeping of a dog in a parked car, which can be a cruel, irresponsible practice in most situations. Dogs have been known to suffer from heat prostration, and worse.

Anti-cruelty laws have also seeped into the world of puppy mills, as more and more of these

Dogs and the Law

unethical outfits are being undermined by concerned owners. The cruel treatment of animals in these farms must be combated by increased legislation. Always know the source of your potential new dog. Avoid sellers who cannot give you all the answers you want to know.

As heart-breaking and unimaginable as it seems, our dogs are not permitted in a great number of places. "No Dog" signs are frequently posted in buildings,

parks, restaurants, motels, etc. It seems that dogs are more accepted in Continental countries, where dogs are permitted (even invited) to dine with the family at a fine restaurant. This not being the case in every American state or city of Great Britain, law-abiding citizens must contend with these restrictions.

Ordinances involving the number of dogs which an owner can keep are prevalent in most communities. These laws vary from place to place and from residency to residency. Whether you live in an apartment, condominium, house, or farm, there may be laws regulating the number of pets you are able to keep. Homes that wish to keep more than the maximum number of animals may be forced to apply for a kennel license or be subject to a daily fine and regular inspection.

For sake of neighbors and the general health of your family, it is wise to take these restrictions to heart. No matter how great your love of animals is, it is not humane to the animals involved to subject them to over-crowding and minimal attention. A small suburban apartment can quickly become the haven of 75 stray dogs and cats, should the owner so choose. Laws such as these prohibit these kinds of communes from blossoming all over the nation.

In most well-organized communities, there are organizations that specialize in Lost and Found dogs. For your dog's safety, you must have the dog licensed and vaccinated, as dogs that are protected in this way have a greater chance of finding their way back home, unscathed. If you

have lost your dog, do not panic, but do work fast. The more people to whom you speak and angles that you take, the greater your chances of retrieving your lost pet. All local authorities (police, fire company, animal control organizations) and all types of media organizations (radio, newspapers, town crier) should be commissioned to lend a hand, keep out a keen eye and ear for the lost dog. Advertising through posters, newspapers, radio, and community lists will pay off in the end. Written descriptions, accompanied by photographs, can assist in helping people have a better mental image of the dog.

Prevention can never be overstressed. Licensing is a must, and the dog must wear the ID tag. Tattoos are quick becoming very popular. These should be located on the dog's inner thigh, not on its ear, as that appendage can easily be torn off by a thief. Tattoos have worked for generations on pack dogs, and the same philosophy of identification can work for pet owners too. Often, the dog's kennel club number or other identifying number is tattooed onto the dog.

Impoundment threatens lost dogs and all other dogs running at large, particularly those without collars and licenses. Most animal control authorities maintain the right to impound, sell, and/or destroy any animal that they catch. As an owner's legal prop-

erty, a dog cannot be impounded or confiscated without the owner's notice. Of course, if the dog is loose and unidentified, the owner is knowingly waiving his rights, and thereby his chances of seeing that the dog has a fair chance to find its way home. A dog that proves itself a nuisance or dangerous to property and people may be confiscated; the owner may be notified ex post facto. An owner may then be invited to court to defend its dog's right to life.

Pounds, as a rule, are required

to keep a dog for a certain period of time before disposing of it in any permanent way. However, this period rarely exceeds four days in length, so owners must act expediently. The fortunate owner who does find his dog at the pound must have the dog vaccinated and licensed (if not done previously), as well as pay a fine. Unclaimed pets are either destroyed humanely or offered for adoption. Many pounds reserve the right to have the owner spay or neuter his unchained canine.

There are also laws that regard the disposal of a dog's remains. Owners must be aware of restrictions in this area. Under certain legislative bodies, a person is not allowed to bury his dog on his own property. In most cases, contacting your family veterinarian or a humane society to handle the details of burial is the most expeditious approach.

DOGS AS PROPERTY

Let there be no doubt about it: a dog is the personal property of its owner. This fact is well substantiated in the various legal codes and statutes under which we all live our daily lives. For dog owners, the dog's legal-property status can be considered a mixed blessing. On the one hand, the dog's legal status as property necessarily guarantees the owner certain rights under the law, the very same rights which pertain to the possession of other property. Homeowners especially should be familiar with some of these rights. On the other hand, the dog's status as legal property places very considerable responsibility on the shoulders of the dog owner, for he will be held legally accountable for the actions of his dog—

Dogs and the Law

just as the homeowner is legally responsible for any injuries that occur on his property and are the result of, for example, negligence resulting from the owner's maintenance of the property.

For the dog owner to be entitled to the rights of a property owner pertinent to his dog, the dog in question must be licensed by the appropriate authorities, usually the local governing body. However, because of the nature of legal systems in most of the free countries, laws may vary from town to town, county to county, and state to state. Thus the owner is strongly encouraged to investigate the necessary requirements

for licensing his dog. At the same time, the owner is encouraged to ascertain the exact nature of the rights of a dog owner under the given laws applicable to the given place of residence.

This varying nature of laws makes it impossible for one to offer details on many of the rights and responsibilities of the dog owner. However, regardless of the place of residence, the dog owner is entitled to due process with regard to the taking of the licensed dog. Due process in this regard refers essentially to the necessary notification of the owner before any further action can be taken by the authorities. In this way, the owner is offered a chance to act on the behalf of his dog, his legal property.

An additional consequence of the legal-property status of the dog is that, as property, the dog cannot be considered a person under the law. One effect of this fact is that the dog therefore cannot be the beneficiary of a will; however, provisions for the care and continued maintenance of the dog can be, and should be, carefully spelled out in the will—just as it would be for the home or any other piece of property.

In summary, the dog is definitely considered property under the law. As such, the dog owner is entitled to given rights and held accountable for given responsibilities. To be granted these rights, the dog owner must license his dog, as well as follow any other guidelines required under the laws of his or her place of residence. Finally, as property, the dog cannot be considered a person, and this fact holds various implications.

Because the dog is the legal property of the dog owner, the dog owner is legally responsible for the behavior of his dog, as well as for the care and maintenance of the animal. However, when the dog is in the possession of a person other than the owner, such as a temporary caretaker, that other person may be held responsible for the dog, depending on the specific circumstances involved and the specific laws of the jurisdiction in which the action(s) occurs. To offer an example, consider the following scenario: A dog is owned by Mr. Smith, who leaves on vacation and hires an individual to care for his dog. While Mr. Smith is on vacation, the dog caretaker walks the dog without a leash and the dog bites a child. Of course, because the dog is property and not person, someone must be held accountable. Should it be Mr. Smith or the caretaker? In such a case it is likely that the caretaker would be held accountable for the dog's biting of the child, provided of course that Mr. Smith did not leave directions to walk the dog without a leash, etc. As we can

Dogs and the Law

see, many variables can come into play regarding legal responsibility for the dog.

To keep it simple in an attempt to offer the reader as much information as possible without getting weighed down in extraneous details, a few general guidelines will be presented.

First, the dog owner, for all intents and purposes, should raise, train, and keep his dog under the assumption that he is legally responsible for every action and for the entire well-being of his dog, ranging from obeying pooper-scooper laws to anti-cruelty laws to dog-bite statutes. In this way, the owner will act as responsibly as possible and, in the end, avoid possible law suits. Secondly, whenever leaving the dog in the custody of others, whether for a short time or a prolonged period, the dog owner should leave clear, explicit written directions regarding proper and appropriate care of the dog. These directions can be prepared ahead of time and kept on file by the owner for use whenever the need arises. In so doing, the owner protects himself in the case of a lawsuit. Thirdly, a minor can be held legally responsible for the dog as property, and this fact needs to be considered whenever a youngster is in charge of the dog. Lastly, the dog owner must familiarize himself with the laws that pertain to him as a dog owner, as a resident of his given community. In no other way can the dog owner act responsibly and thus be protected under the law.

Because the dog owner is legally responsible for his dog, he is liable for all damages and personal injuries that result from the dog. Under strict liability, the owner is liable for any damages or injury caused by the dog, even if they are not the "fault" of the owner. Of course, common law doctrines are the products of court decisions, and thus may vary from place to place. Additionally,

liability may be subject to the same circumstantial variables as those which apply to responsibility in general.

Because the owner is liable for the actions of his dog, he can be taken to court and sued. A person injured by a dog will likely receive reimbursement for all medical expenses, as well as a given sum for pain and suffering, depending on the circumstances. The same conditions apply to damages: a person can receive full reimbursement for the loss or damage of any property that was the product of the dog's actions. In serious cases, e.g., those involving blatant negligence, malice or forethought,

Dogs and the Law

the owner of the dog can be sentenced to prison and/or fined.

The subject of vicious dogs abounds in controversy, in part because of the lack of an all-encompassing definition of viciousness as it pertains to the dog and in part because there is a current trend to label entire breeds of dog as inherently vicious. Because of the controversial nature of the vicious-dog subject, the reader is encouraged to do two things: first, read up on the specific laws pertaining to canine viciousness that apply to his locale; and second, to employ utmost common sense in the execution of his dog-owning responsibilities. The first step is by far the easier of the two, for vicious-dog statutes can be found in most libraries and at many municipal buildings. Beginning with inquiries and following up with research ensures the dog owner expedient acquisition of the applicable laws regarding viciousness and his dog. The second step, regarding the application of common sense to all aspects of canine ownership, requires that the dog owner first obey all laws pertinent to his ownership, e.g., leash laws, proper training, housing, restriction, etc.; second be well aware and understand the nature of his charge and adjust its keeping accordingly; and lastly take all steps necessary to ensure that others who may care for the dog be explicitly instructed on how to execute their caretaker task.

By following the two-step process just described to help you guard against a potential vicious-dog law suit, especially in following the application of common sense to your dog ownership, you to a large degree also work to prevent injury, both to yourself and to others. In so doing, you are also necessarily limiting the possibility that you will find yourself beside your dog in court over your dog's injuring another person.

To assist the dog owner in applying common sense to his dog ownership, the following principles are presented: (1) all dogs, meaning each and every dog, no matter how small or large a dog, young or old a dog, has the potential to injure a person; (2) dogs act largely on instinct and perceive the world much differently than people do, i.e., a dog may see a situation as dangerous and react with fear biting even though a person sees the situation as perfectly non-threatening or even pleasant; (3) not all people are dog fanciers, and some people even delight in provoking and taunting an animal, which can easily lead to their being injured; (4) dogs do not treat all people in the same manner as they treat you, their owner and caretaker.

By considering these principles, obeying the laws of dog ownership (which essentially are designed for the protection of you, your dog, and others), and consistently applying common sense in your daily doggie doings, you by and large prevent injury.

In recent years, insurance companies have offered insurance policies to dog owners. Essentially these policies can be grouped into two general categories: canine life insurance and liability insurance. Of course, many different policies from each category are offered, and the cost of the respective policy varies roughly in accordance with the coverage offered. For example, a "life" insurance policy that covered accidental injury as well as providing a death benefit will typically cost more

than a policy that offers only a death benefit, provided of course that the death benefits are of equivalent value.

Canine insurance is not for every dog owner, though every dog owner is encouraged to investigate the various policies offered and for themselves make the determination of whether yea or nay they purchase such insurance. Common consensus offers that canine insurance is best suited for two kinds of dog owners, a splitting that roughly corresponds to the two kinds of canine insurance offered. The first kind of owner is the professional breeder

Dogs and the Law

and/or showperson, who has invested large sums of money in his individual dogs and stands to lose much in the case of accidental injury or death. Such a person is strongly encouraged to investigate the canine life insurance available. In short, he is encouraged to protect his investment. The second type of person is the owner of a guard dog or any dog trained or demonstrating the proclivity to attack a person. For this dog owner, investigation of some type of liability insurance is encouraged.

After all is said and done, after all steps and measures towards responsible lawful ownership have been taken, there may still come a time when the dog owner finds himself in the midst of a controversy. The cause may be a very simple or insignificant one, or it may be a very complex one. The important point to remember is that a controversy must be managed in a legal and responsible way.

If the controversy is a minor one, it might be best to attempt to resolve the the problem between the two parties, in which case a third party (an objective mediator) often proves helpful. If this fails for any reason, e.g., tempers, then going to the authorities is strongly recommended. In no case should anyone attempt to take matters into their own hands, becoming judge, jury, and executioner all in one. If the controversy involves a serious matter, you are encouraged to seek legal advice as soon as possible. Remember that you are responsible for the actions of your dog, and therefore you can be held liable for any damages or injuries that your dog may inflict. All controversies should be approached in an objective manner; the dog owner must realize that there are at least two sides to the story and that resolution of the conflict will likely involve at least small compromises from each of the parties involved.

CRUELTY

What determines or defines cruelty to animals often excites great controversy in our society.

Anti-cruelty legislation, nonetheless, continues to make headway, as new laws are being enforced with regularity. Avoiding the inhumane treatment of animals, neglect and abuse should be the target of all caring dog owners. The conditions of a breeding facility or animal shelter, cosmetic alterations of puppies (cropping ears and docking tails), protocol for dealing with an injured animal, and impoundment of lost, vicious or destructive dogs are just some of the topics which anti-cruelty laws address. In the United States, ear cropping and tail docking are not prohibited as they are in Great Britain. Britain has for generations deemed such cosmetic alterations unnecessary and unnecessarily cruel.

TRAVEL

When traveling with your dog, there are a number of considerations with which to be concerned. The most common method of travel is automobiles, though fewer laws address this mode of transportation. Regarding urban travel, i.e., buses, subways, rails, dogs are usually not permitted on board unless the dog is an assistance dog. Some railways allow dogs to stay in the owner's cabin, while others require that the dog be kept in the baggage compartment (likely there is an area especially equipped for live cargo). Always check with the railway and train station about the regulations regarding your dog. Do this before leaving home! If you intend to travel by sea, less common in today's world of airplanes, it is advised that similar inquiries be made to the ship's station.

Air travel can be a more difficult matter. Airlines most usually allow dogs to fly on their flights. Small dogs can be carried on, while large ones need to be kept in the baggage area. Of course the appropriate crate is required for any dog traveling by air. Mark the crate: "Live Cargo" or "This End Up" for the safety of your canine luggage. Travel agents are usually well informed and will advise you on such decisions.

LANDLORDS AND DOGS

Regardless of how it may seem, there is no *natural* antipathy between landlords and dogs. Dogs in themselves are no more the natural enemy of landlords than, say, tenants are. Landlords and dogs don't get along for the most part because in many cases dogs and tenants—both dog owners and non-dog owners—don't get along. Landlords often try to outlaw the ownership of dogs by their tenants simply because dogs make trouble. They can be destructive, they can make messes, they can scare people, they can hurt people. To avoid the trouble that dogs can make, landlords write into their leases clauses that prohibit the keeping of dogs by tenants. Landlords in general might not be the nicest people in the world, but you can't blame them for wanting to avoid trouble and expense that tenants' pet dogs may bring them. For

example, would you as landlord relish the idea of being sued by some troublemaking yardbird who, while visiting one of your tenants, was bitten by his homicidal cur? And don't ask why he'd be suing the landlord when it wasn't the landlord's dog that bit him—he'd be suing everyone in sight, as the courts encourage that type of madness: wouldn't a reasonably prudent landlord provide 24-hour guard service to make sure that visitors are not attacked in their buildings?

Governmental units at various levels are telling landlords that they can't tell their tenants not to own dogs (or cats), and various courts are starting to tell landlords that either their leases don't say what they plainly do say or that they say it but the courts don't like it and will therefore come up with a reason why it shouldn't be allowed. But the milennium for dog-owning apartment dwellers has not yet arrived; until it does, the best thing a tenant can do is to ask for permission from the owner...and to get it in writing.

Index

Age, 43
Aggressiveness, 105
Aging process,
    135–136
AKC, 47
Balls, 85, 118
Barking, 101–104
Bed, 69, 70–71
Breeder's contract,
    153
Calculus, 147, 149
Canine hepatitis, 129
Caries, dental, 138
Castration, 42, 170
Chewing need, 138
Chew toys, 115–119
Children, 44, 52
Confinement, 71, 72
Crate, 71–73, 111,
    189
Destructive behavior,
    110–111, 142
Development of
    puppy, 171
Distemper, 128, 138
Dog house, 69, 74–76
Dominance, 105
Ear mites, 127
Estrus, 155–158
Evolution of dog, 35
Feeding, chart, 68;
    commercial foods,
    60; routine, 65
Fertilization, 157
Fetching, 80–83
First aid kit, 119
Fleas, 133–134
Flossing, 143
Frisbee®, 80–83
Gestation, 162
Gumabone®, as chew
    product, 51; as
    exercise tool, 117;
    as therapeutic
    device, 147,

150–152
Gumadisc®, 81
Heartworms, 135; life
    cycle, 136
Hookworms, 134–135
Housebreaking, 87–90
Illness, signs, 127;
    symptoms, 113
Inoculations, 52, 128
Kennel Club of Great
    Britain, 47
Kennel cough, 132
Leptospirosis, 129
License, 48, 173–174
Life span, 42, 43
Lyme disease,
    131–132
Mosquito bites, 136
Muzzle, 104, 123, 174,
    182
Neutering, 153, 170
Nursing, 167
Nylabone®, 51, 70,
    111, 142, 143
Nylafloss®, 142, 143
Nylon chews, 141–142
Nylon discs, 80
Nylon toys, 115–117
Old dogs, 135–137
Ovulation, 156
Pack instincts, 105
Paper training, 89
Parainfluenza, 132
Parasites, 77,
    133–135
Parvovirus, 130–131
Pedigree papers, 46,
    47
Periodontitis, 146
Plaque, 147, 149
Plaque Attacker®, 118
Poisoning, 119–120
Polyurethane toys, 81,
    117
Pregnancy, 162

Punishment, 95
Purchase, 42–44
Rabies, 129–131
Rawhide, 140–141
Registration, 46, 48
Roundworms, 134
Selection, 42–44
Shock, 126
Show quality, 37, 153
Socialization, 171
Spaying, 43, 153, 170
Supplements, food,
    62; vitamin and
    mineral, 63, 162
Tapeworm, 134–135
Tartar, 138
Temperature, sign of
    labor, 164; body,
    113
Territory, male's, 158
Ticks, 132, 134–135
Tooth care, 138—151
Toys, 115–119
Training, 90–100;
    Come, 98; Down,
    99; Heel, 97; Sit,
    96; Stay, 96
Travel, 123, 188
Tug toys, 82
Ultra Rubber®, 81–82
United Kennel Club,
    47
Vaccination, 128, 174
Veterinary care, 51,
    112
Vitamins, 63, 162
Weaning, 167–170
Whelping, 162,
    164–166; box, 161;
    chart, 152
Whipworms, 134–135
Worming, 134, 169

Dog Breeding for Professionals
By Dr. Herbert Richards (H-969)

For dog owners who need and actively seek good advice about how to go about breeding their dogs whether for profit or purely because of their attachment to animals. *Please note* that the breeding photography is sexually explicit and some readers may find it offensive.

Hard cover, 5.5 in x 8 in, 224 pages, 105 black and white photos, 62 color photos.
ISBN 0-87666-659-4a

Dog Training
By Lew Burke (H-962)

The elements of dog training are easy to grasp and apply. The author uses the psychological makeup of dogs to his advantage by making them want to be what they should be—substituting the family for the pack.

Hard cover, 5.5 in x 8 in, 255 pages, 64 black and white photos, 23 color photos.
ISBN 0-87666-656-X

The Mini Atlas of Dog Breeds
By Andrew De Prisco & James B. Johnson (H-1106)

An identification handbook giving a concise and thorough look at over 400 of the world's dog breeds. The authors' enthusiastic and knowledgeable approach brings to life instantly man's oldest friend and companion. A flowing and witty text, further enlivened by 500 full-color photos, successfully maps out the world of dogs; an easy-reference format pinpoints each breed's development, portrait, registry, and

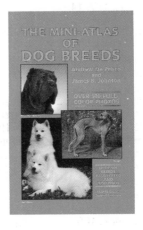

pet attributes. The volume is captioned with specially designed symbols.

Hard cover, 5.5 in x 8.5 in, 544 pages, nearly 700 color photos.
ISBN 0-86622-091-7

Dog Owner's Encyclopedia of Veterinary Medicine
By Allan H. Hart, B.V.Sc. (H-934)

Written by a vet who feels that most dog owners should recognize the symptoms and understand the cures of most diseases of dogs so they can properly communicate with their veterinarian. This book is a necessity for every dog owner, especially those who have more than one dog. *Hard cover, 5.5 in x 8 in, 186 pages, 86 black and white photos. ISBN 0-87666-287-4*

The Proper Care of Dogs
By Christopher Burris (TW-102)
Discusses the basic care of all dogs and highlights the specific needs of every A.K.C.—recog-

nized breed. Ideal for the prospective dog owner, this compact and colorful book lays the groundwork for general canine management and provides an overview of the world of dogs. *Hard cover, 5 in x 7 in, 256 pages, over 200 full-color photos. ISBN 0-86622-402-5*

The Atlas of Dog Breeds of the World
By Bonnie Wilcox, DVM, & Chris Walkowicz (H-1091)

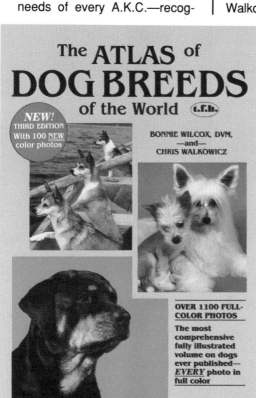

The ATLAS of
DOG BREEDS
of the World t.f.h.

NEW!
THIRD EDITION
With 100 NEW
color photos

BONNIE WILCOX, DVM,
—and—
CHRIS WALKOWICZ

OVER 1100 FULL-COLOR PHOTOS

The most comprehensive fully illustrated volume on dogs ever published— *EVERY* photo in full color

Traces the history and highlights the characteristics, appearance and function of every recognized dog breed in the world. 409 different breeds receive full-color treatment and individual study. Hundreds of breeds in addition to those recognized by the American Kennel Club and the Kennel Club of Great Britain are included—the dogs of the world complete! The ultimate reference work, comprehensive coverage, intelligent and delightful discussions. The perfect gift book. *Hard cover, 9 in x 12 in, 912 pages, 1,106 color photos. ISBN 0-86622-930-2*